THOMAS ALVA EDISON

LIVES TO REMEMBER

Thomas Alva Edison

by Henry Thomas

ILLUSTRATED BY ANDRE LE BLANC

FOUNDED 1838

GPPS

66894

G. P. PUTNAM'S SONS
NEW YORK

Library of Congress Catalog

Card Number: 58-7457

Published simultaneously in the Dominion of Canada

by Longmans, Green and Company, Toronto.

MANUFACTURED IN THE UNITED STATES OF AMERICA

VAN REES PRESS • NEW YORK

CONTENTS

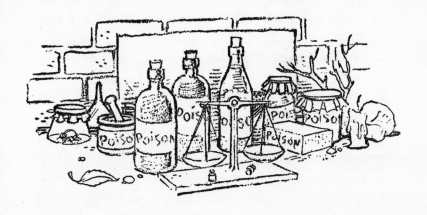

Chapter 1

QUICK TO THINK, SLOW TO QUIT

THOMAS ALVA EDISON was a genius with an amazing ability to size up a situation. One day, when he was working on his discovery of electric light, he wanted to get the measurement of the inside of an irregular glass bulb. Being busy with his own work, he asked one of his brightest assistants to help him.

The young man, who was an expert in mathematics, armed himself with many sheets of paper and sat down at his desk. About a week later, Edison asked him whether he was making any progress.

"Yes, sir," said the assistant, "but I am not yet finished."

Edison looked at the work. It covered several pages

of charts and figures. "How much longer will it take?" he asked.

"Another week or so, Mr. Edison."

"But the whole thing can be done in a minute," said Edison. "Let me show you how."

He filled the bulb with water.

"Now pour the water into a measuring cup, and you've got the answer."

Together with his astonishing power of observation, Edison had an equally astonishing capacity for taking pains. In his vocabulary he had no place for the word *quit*. He could work for weeks and months and even years on a single invention.

During his experiments on the storage battery, he had made about ten thousand tests with different chemical combinations, and all of them had proved unsuccessful. Again and again he was told that he would never find the right combination. Even his closest friends began to feel that he was wasting his time. "Isn't it a pity," said one of them, "that with all this effort you haven't discovered a single thing that will work?"

"But," retorted Edison, "I've discovered ten thousand things that will not work. So I am closer than ever to the goal."

And before long he reached it, as he did with almost everything else he undertook.

Edison inherited his mental and physical powers from a sturdy stock of pioneers. His great-grandfather, John Edison, had been threatened with hanging as a British sympathizer in the Revolutionary War. But he had made his escape from Staten Island to Nova Scotia. His grandfather, Samuel Edison, had migrated from Nova Scotia to Canada. And his father, Samuel Edison Junior, had moved back from Canada to the United States.

The Edisons were always on the go—either to escape from old hardships or to seek new opportunities for a better life. The reason for the migration of Edison's father back to the States was his desire to improve things, not only for himself but also for his country. He had been forced to flee from Canada because he was involved in a plan to overthrow the Tory government and to replace it with a representative government like that of the United States. He was a giant of a man, with long legs and a stout heart. Indeed it was his long legs, he said, that had carried him across the trackless forests and the icebound rivers, until he found safety in the village of Milan, Ohio.

Through the help of a friendly barge captain by the name of Alva Bradley, Samuel Edison sent for his wife and his six children, who had stayed behind in Canada. When the family was reunited, he set up a mill for making shingles and started upon a new life.

And it was here in Milan, during a blizzard on February 11, 1847, that his seventh child was born. Friends of the family predicted that the baby would lead an active life, for he had been blown into the world on the wings of the wind. His parents named him Thomas Alva Edison—the middle name in honor of Mr. Alva Bradley. And they pronounced the last name Ead-i-son.

It was not until several years later that the pronunciation was changed to Ed-i-son.

From his earliest childhood Alva—or Al, as his family called him—was full of restless activity and original thoughts. He was always ready "to learn something about everything." He tried his first "scientific experiment" at the age of six, when he set his father's barn on fire to see what would happen. The result was not quite what he had expected. The barn burned down to the ground, almost burning Alva along with it, and his father paid him for his curiosity by giving him a public spanking in the village square.

On another occasion, he tried to hatch a number of birds by sitting on a nest of goose eggs. All he succeeded in hatching was a mess of scrambled eggs on the seat of his trousers, another spanking, and another discovery of things that would not work.

When he was seven, his parents moved to Port Huron, Michigan. And here, too, Alva went on with his experiments, often to his parents' annoyance and his own disappointment. His father called him the "nervous little question mark." He was continually seeking information from others and trying to find out things for himself.

One of the things that bothered him, for example, was the secret of a bird's flight. He asked his father about it but received no satisfactory answer. So he concluded that the birds were able to fly because they ate worms.

He followed this strange thought with speedy action.

If a bird could fly by eating worms, why couldn't their hired girl do the same?

Accordingly, he prepared a concoction of water and worms and prevailed upon the hired girl to drink it. Instead of flying through the air, the poor girl fell to the ground in an agony of pain. Fortunately, she quickly recovered from the experiment. But it cost Edison his supper.

Yet his hunger for experiments remained as keen as his hunger for food. Still curious about the secret of flight, he tried another kind of test upon one of his playmates, Michael Oates. He gave him a big dose of Seidlitz powders to lift him into the air like an inflated balloon. Again the only results were a stomach ache for Michael and a spanking for Alva.

But still he kept at it. "The only way to find out is to try."

His father, with an eye to business, had built upon his grounds an observation tower overlooking Lake Huron and the St. Clair River. The admission charge for a view of the panorama from the top of the tower was twenty-five cents. The venture was not a success, but it continued to attract one "customer" for a long time. Again and again, young Alva climbed to the top and through an old telescope gazed upon the steamboats and the sailing ships that skimmed over the waters of the lake. And thus his thoughts kept expanding toward the horizon and beyond.

Alva had another favorite retreat—the underground cellar of the Edison house. In this cellar he had gathered a collection of bottles, jars, chemicals, odd insects, plants and rocks he had picked up on his rambles through the woods. He spent much of his spare time in his cellar laboratory, performing all sorts of experiments that kept crowding into his active brain. His mother had presented him with a copy of Richard Green Parker's *School of Natural Philosophy*—a treasurehouse of practical wonders for the young inventor. He was only nine, yet he plunged into the book with a determination to master it from beginning to end.

And he did master it. Many of his childhood experiments were based upon the knowledge he had picked up from this book. In order to keep the other children away from his precious bottles and jars, he marked them POISON.

His mother, who had taught school, realized that Alva had an unusual mind. But his teacher at the Port Huron school could see in him nothing but an inattentive child with a faraway look in his eyes. One day, only three months after the beginning of term, the teacher remarked to the supervisor that Alva was "addled" and "not worth the time wasted on him."

Alva overheard this remark and later burst into tears when he came home and reported it to his mother. Mrs. Edison went to the school and indignantly told the teacher that he did not know what he was talking about. From that day on, she undertook to teach Alva herself.

Alva became an object of envy to the other children as they saw him and his mother on the front porch. Mrs. Edison, a charming woman in a black dress and a lace cap, would be reading to the boy in a gentle voice—so different from the scolding tones of their school-teacher. Mother and son looked very much alike. They had the same plump cheeks, deep blue eyes, and full lips always ready to break into a smile.

Mrs. Edison did an excellent job as Alva's teacher. Coming from a family of ministers, she was able to provide her child with a knowledge of the three R's, as well as to inspire him with a love for God, a respect for all sorts of people, and a hunger to learn as many facts about as many things as possible. By the time he was ten, she had guided him to the reading of such books as Gibbon's *Decline and Fall of the Roman Empire,* Hume's *History of England,* Sear's *History of the World,* and the *Dictionary of Sciences.* He probably didn't understand everything he read in these books, but he got out of them a lifelong habit of deep and serious thinking.

His reading, his studies and his experiments took much, but not all, of his time. His father saw to that. He made Alva help him with the planting and the hoeing of his vegetable garden.

But all this was not enough for Alva. He wanted to get a job in order to earn enough money for his experiments. He saw his chance when the railroad people opened a new line running from Port Huron to Detroit. He was only twelve, but he was ready to launch into competition with the grown-up world.

One day he spoke to his mother about his plan. She felt that he was much too young, and his father agreed with her. But the boy refused to budge, and finally they gave in. "Provided," said his father, "the railroad authorities will be foolish enough to listen to you."

Alva wrote to them, offering his services without pay. All he asked of them was permission to sell newspapers and fruits and candy to the passengers, and to keep whatever profits he might make.

At first he failed to get the job. "Too young." But to Edison, failure was but another spur to persistence. He tried again, and again, until finally the railroad people decided to take him on.

So Thomas Alva Edison, a boy of twelve, had entered upon his first gigantic task. A business of his own on a speeding train, away from his family for several hours a day. No wonder his mother was afraid.

But there was no fear in Edison's heart.

Chapter 2

THE MERCHANT-STUDENT

IT WAS Edison's plan to earn in order to learn. Averaging a profit of about four dollars a day on his sales, he gave one dollar to his mother and spent the other three dollars on scientific books and chemical equipment. He had set up a laboratory in the corner of the baggage car, and here during his spare time he was to be found experimenting.

But this wasn't all. Every day he had six and a half hours of free time in Detroit. The train left Port Huron at 7 in the morning, arriving in Detroit at 10; it left Detroit on the return trip at 4:30 in the afternoon, arriving in Port Huron at 7:30. It didn't take Edison long to find out what he could do with those free hours in Detroit. He spent most of them in the library.

15

At first he thought of reading all the sixteen thousand volumes on the shelves, beginning with A and ending with Z. But in time he realized that this was too much of an undertaking. He decided to select only those books that would be most helpful in his scientific studies.

Let us now have a closer look at the little merchant-student as he peddles his goods on the train. He is of average height, broad shoulders, blue eyes, uncombed brown hair pushing out helter-skelter from underneath a white cap worn at an angle over his right eye. A white coat opened at the front and a clean shirt under-neath—his mother saw to that every morning—but his trousers were unpressed and his shoes unshined. In spite of his mother's scolding, he never learned to be tidy.

A curious but lovable fellow. The passengers would go out of their way to do him favors. And he was always up to something new. When the huckleberries ripened in the woods around Port Huron, he bought them at a low price and sold them at a handsome profit in Detroit. He even opened a fruit stall of his own to take care of the unsold goods. And when the business got too big for him to handle by himself, he hired other boys to help him.

All in all, Edison found his peddling on the rail-road and the managing of his fruit stand in Detroit rather profitable. But he was not satisfied. His busy mind kept probing for new channels of activity. So he added another venture to his business interests. He started a newspaper of his own, and he named it the *Weekly Herald*.

He had picked up the printing press secondhand in a stationery store. It was a rickety thing but good enough for his purpose. He became the reporter, copyreader, editor, printer and circulation manager of the paper, and he did all this work in the baggage car. He was not only the youngest publisher in America—fifteen years old—but the owner of the one newspaper in the world printed on a train.

It was a small paper, about the size of a handkerchief, and it consisted of only a single sheet. Yet it often contained news "hot off the wire," for Edison had friends among the telegraph operators who worked at the railroad stations. He was able to get from them the latest news items before they got into the other papers.

Edison had a knack for taking advantage of the important happenings of the day. And, at least on one occasion, this knack helped him to sell his regular papers at a handsome profit. It was on the day of the Union Army victory in the Battle of Shiloh, April 7, 1862. Edison had made arrangements with a printer on the Detroit *Free Press* to let him see the galley proofs of the important stories before they were printed in the paper. On the day of the victory, Edison read the news while the ink was still wet on the galley sheets.

As soon as he was finished with the reading, he rushed to the railroad station and asked the telegraph operator to wire the news to every train stop along the line, together with a statement that the full details would be published in the newspapers later on.

He then hurried to Mr. William F. Storey, the editor

of the *Free Press,* and asked him for a thousand papers instead of the two hundred that he sold on ordinary days. "I haven't got the money now, sir," he said, "but I'll pay for them tomorrow."

Mr. Storey, pleased with the boy's energy, granted his request.

Edison got one of the boys at the office to help him with the big bundle and rushed over to the train. The first stop after Detroit was Utica, about twelve miles away. Here he generally sold two papers. Today, he thought, he might dispose of six. Looking out the window as the train pulled into the station, he rubbed his eyes in amazement. The platform was crowded with people who had read the announcement of the victory on the bulletin board and who were clamoring for the paper that would give them the entire story. He sold forty papers at Utica.

Whereupon Edison raised the price of the paper to five cents.

At the next stop, Mount Clemens, he sold a hundred and fifty copies, and then raised the price to ten cents.

By the time he reached Port Huron, he had only a few papers left. He disposed of them at twenty-five cents a copy, keeping one paper for his parents. This he proudly presented to them, together with nearly a hundred dollars that he had made on his clever scoop.

Although young Edison's business kept increasing almost daily, he still found plenty of time for his experiments. One of these experiments, however, proved very costly. He was trying out a new chemical in the baggage car when the train went speeding around a high curve. A stick of phosphorus fell to the floor and burst into flame. While Edison was trying to put it out, the fire spread and soon the entire floor was in a blaze.

The conductor of the train, Alexander Stevenson, was a man of quick action. He rushed into the baggage car, seized a bucket of water, extinguished the fire, and then turned on Edison. "Out you go at the next stop!"

And when the train arrived at a crossing called Smith's Creek, Edison found himself out on the platform, together with his workbench, printing press and laboratory equipment.

Later on, he was allowed to come back to work on the train. But his experiments in the baggage car were at an end. From that time on, he was obliged to do his experimenting at home. Not, however, in the cellar. His new workroom was the attic. "We feel safer with you over us than under us," said his father. "If you blow up the attic, the lower floors will remain. But if you blow up the cellar, the entire house will explode."

Chapter 3

A TELEGRAM IS LIKE A LONG DOG

IN ADDITION to his chemical studies, Alva Edison became interested in telegraphy. As a result of Professor Morse's invention, thousands of boys were experimenting with the "miracle of flying messages." Alva took every opportunity to get information about this miracle from the telegraph operators at the railroad stations.

"How does electricity carry a message through the air?" he would ask.

Nobody could give him a satisfactory answer. But one of the operators succeeded in firing his imagination.

"A telegram," he said, "is like a long dog with its tail in Boston and its head in Chicago. You pull its tail at one end, and it barks at the other end."

"Yes, but what brings the message from the tail to the head?"

"I don't know."

Edison decided to try for himself. One day, when the train had stopped at a station, he prevailed upon the conductor to hold the front paws of the telegraph operator's dog while the operator held the hind legs. Then he took into his own right hand a wire which he had stretched from the baggage car, and with his left he grasped the conductor's free hand. There was an electric shock that made everybody jump. When the station master rushed out of his office those involved in the experiment had fled from the scene.

So Edison escaped another scolding, but he went on with his experiments in telegraphy. He had a young friend, Jim Clancy, who lived about half a mile from the Edison home. Together the two boys strung up a line of stovepipe wire between their houses. They used bottles and rags for insulators, and pieces of brass for keys. For the electric current they first tried a number of cats. They hoped to generate the current by vigorously rubbing their fur. But all they succeeded in generating was a series of yowls, scratches and bites. They gave up the cats and turned to homemade batteries, from which they succeeded in creating enough "juice" to work their instruments.

Delighted with their success. the two boys worked

until late at night, sending messages to each other in the Morse code of dots and dashes. When this had gone on for several days, Edison's father put his foot down. "You've got to get up early to catch your train. So stop fooling with that contraption and go to bed. Eleven sharp every night, do you understand?"

This was a terrible blow to Edison. As a rule he stayed out till eleven trying to dispose of the papers that were left over from the sales on the train. Obeying his father's command would leave him no time for his experiments with Jim Clancy.

But he quickly found a way out of the difficulty. He recalled that he always brought the unsold papers for his father to read at night. Why not wire the news to him instead? With this germ of an idea, he enlisted the help of Jim Clancy and set to work.

One night he came home without any papers, and explained to his father that he had sold all of them with the exception of one copy that he had left with Jim's folks. "But I'll tell you what, father. I'll get the news for you from Jim, over our telegraph line."

His father, seeing through the ruse, consented with a smile. Alva went to his instrument and sent a wire to Jim, asking him to telegraph the news, bit by bit, so that he himself could transcribe it on paper and give it to his father. This turned out to be such a slow process that it was one o'clock before they were able to go to bed.

The next night, and the night after that, Edison repeated the trick. At last his father surrendered. "Very well," he said, "from now on you can bring the papers and stay up as long as you please."

Edison's knowledge of telegraphy, combined with his ability to think fast, proved to be a blessing to his townspeople on one important occasion. An ice jam had broken down the wires between Port Huron and Canada, and the operators found it impossible to send any messages across the lake. But Edison, as usual, thought of an ingenious plan. "I can send the messages for you," he said, "if you will give me a locomotive and an engineer." The railroad authorities smiled—another "crazy" scheme of his, perhaps—but they granted his request. And then Edison went to work with a plan as simple as it was ingenious. He tooted out a telegraph message in Morse code on the engine whistle. There was no answer at first, but after a while a Canadian operator understood and tooted back a message in reply. And thus they used their temporary telegraph service until the wires were repaired. "This boy," said everybody, "has a wonderful future ahead of him."

He went on with his study of telegraphy and, thanks to the experts at the railroad stations, made rapid progress. They were ready to help him at every opportunity. This was especially true of Jim Mackenzie, the station master and telegraph operator at Mount Clemens.

Mackenzie's fondness for Edison was the result of Alva's quick mind and unusual courage. One summer morning when the train had stopped at Mount Clemens to take on water, Edison stood on the platform chatting with Mackenzie. Suddenly, to his horror, he saw little Jimmy, Mackenzie's two-year-old son, playing on the tracks in the path of an onrushing train. Edison dropped his papers, dashed down the tracks, and rescued the child from certain death.

"I have no money to offer you," said the father, overcome with joy, "but I'll tell you what I'll do. I'll make you one of the best telegraph operators in the country, and then I'll get you a job."

And Mackenzie kept his promise. Within three months he taught Edison all he knew about telegraphy. And Edison absorbed this knowledge as quickly as it was given to him. By now he was a gangling, untidy but brilliant youngster of sixteen, ready to enter upon his new job.

But before he left his old job on the train, he met with an accident that was to cause him trouble for the rest of his life. As he was trying to sell his papers on the station platform at Smith's Creek, he saw the train pulling out and made a dash for the nearest car. He missed it and was in danger of falling under the wheels, when the conductor seized him by the ears and lifted him into the train. Edison felt something snap in his head. From that day on, he was partially deaf.

In later years Edison regarded this affliction as a possible blessing in disguise. "It keeps away the noises of the world," he said, "and it allows me to concentrate on my work." Like the composer Beethoven, who was deaf when he wrote his greatest music, Edison learned to listen with his "inner ear." Sometimes nature allows genius to develop out of pain, just as it makes the flowers grow out of the dirt. Edison realized this fact, and he never complained about his handicap. It was merely another spur to harder work.

Chapter 4

THE VAGABOND TELEGRAPH
OPERATOR

EDISON—who was now called Tom instead of Alva—began his work as a telegraph operator at Stratford Junction, a Canadian town not far from Port Huron. It was a night job, and it paid him only twenty-five dollars a month—just a fraction of what he had earned as a newsboy on the train. But he cared little for money. He was much more interested in learning, inventing, and doing things that were worth while.

But his very first invention was not at all worth while, for it cost him his job. This is how it happened:

He worked each night from 7 in the evening to 7 in the morning. Days were spent mostly in experimenting instead of sleeping. He had rented a room in a boardinghouse, and he had set up a laboratory in one of its corners.

After a day's experiments in the laboratory he was often so tired that he dozed off at his desk in the telegraph office. But the operators were not allowed to sleep on the job. Once every hour the main office required them to flash the letter "A" as a signal that they were awake.

Edison sought an answer to his problem, and his ingenious mind soon found it. He invented a clock that would send the hourly signal for him, while he slept. It was a simple contraption. To an ordinary alarm clock he attached a revolving wheel, together with a lever that rested upon the letter "A" in the telegraph instrument. Whenever the clock struck the hour, the wheel opened the circuit and the lever flashed the signal over the wire. Edison took care to silence the bell of the alarm clock, so that he was able to sleep in peace while the clock did its work.

For several nights the invention worked beautifully. But at last the chief telegraph operator at Toronto became suspicious. The signals were coming in exactly on the hour, not a minute too early or too late. This seemed strange to him, for Edison was not that punctual. One night he decided to send a wire to Edison right after he received the signal. He got no response to his wire and became alarmed. Perhaps the poor boy had fainted, or even died! He rushed to the Stratford station—and found Edison sound asleep.

And then he saw the clever invention. For a moment

he smiled, for he admired Edison. But his sense of duty got the better of his admiration. A sleeping operator might cause a lot of trouble when an important message was on the wire. He shook Tom awake. "Sorry, Edison, but you're fired!"

Edison got another job at a nearby station; but this job, too, was short-lived. One night he received an order over the wire to halt a freight train. Wiring back that he would do so, he hurried out only to see that he was too late. The freight train was roaring past the station.

He rushed back into the office, flashed the news to head off any train that might be coming in the opposite direction, and then plunged after the freight train through the darkness. In his panic he imagined a head-on collision, dead and wounded people, wreckage strewn all over the tracks, and heaven knows what else! . . . He lost his footing and fell down a steep bank.

He was knocked unconscious. When he opened his eyes, he learned that fortunately there had been no disaster. The freight train and another train speeding from the opposite direction had come to a stop because the two engineers had seen the headlights just in time.

But there was trouble in store for Tom. He was summoned to the office of W. J. Spicer, the general manager in Toronto, to be tried for neglect of duty. "Young man," said Mr. Spicer, "we could send you to the penitentiary for this . . ."

Tom was about to explain that it was really not his fault when a couple of important visitors from England came in to see the general manager. In the excitement of the visit, Tom shot out of the office and boarded a freight train that carried him safely out of Canada and back to the United States.

Edison had now become a vagabond, drifting from city to city in search of a new start. He didn't look very likely—hair straggling over his head, paper collar without any tie, and the usual unpressed clothes. But he found it easy to get jobs because many of the telegraphers were at the front fighting in the Civil War.

Most of the jobs lasted only a short time. Sometimes a manager would dismiss him in favor of a relative or a friend. At other times a superintendent would order Tom to leave because he "spent too much time on dreaming and too little time on working." And on one occasion he incurred the anger of his chief because he interrupted one of the chief's messages with another message that Tom regarded as more important. For in those days it was not possible to send two telegrams together over a single wire.

Edison was only seventeen when he offended this chief. He lost his job—but he got an idea. If the crowding of a wire meant the loss of a job, why not find a way to uncrowd it? Why couldn't he invent a machine that would send more than one telegram over the same wire at the same time?

At the moment, however, he was too busy looking for a new job. Later on, perhaps, but not now. So he traveled from place to place—Detroit, Indianapolis, Cincinnati, Fort Wayne, Memphis, New Orleans—even plan-

ning a trip to South America. He was about to leave for Vera Cruz with two other young men, when he was persuaded at the last moment to stay behind. It was a fortunate thing that he did, for his two friends were stricken there with yellow fever and died.

He had another narrow escape from death when, in the course of his wanderings, he came to Cincinnati. But Edison tells this story in his own words:

While a telegraph operator in Cincinnati, I was as great a reader as in the old days; and my salary being small, I used to wander among the auction-rooms and pick up a bargain whenever I got the chance.

One day there was put up to the highest bidder a stack of *North American Reviews,* and I secured a lot for two dollars. I carried the parcel—which was heavy enough to put on a truck—to the telegraph office, arriving there just in time to report. At three A.M. I was free. Shouldering my package, I went down the dark street at a lively pace.

Presently I heard a pistol shot behind me and something whizzed past my ear, nearly grazing it in fact. As I turned, a breathless policeman came up and ordered me to drop my parcel. Evidently hurrying along the dark alley with my bundle, I did look rather suspicious.

I stopped and opened my package. The policeman looked disgusted. "Why didn't you halt when I told you?" he said. "If I'd been a better shot you might have got killed." He apologized afterwards when I explained to him that it was because of my deafness that I hadn't obeyed his commands.

Edison continued his wanderings for a time and then, at the age of twenty-one, found his way to Boston. He had sent an application for a job to George F. Milliken, the superintendent of the Western Union station in that city. It was winter when he arrived, and Edison was almost frozen stiff from the cold. His train had been snowbound for three days in a blizzard but he still managed to walk briskly into the Western Union office and stride up to Milliken's desk.

"What can I do for you?" asked Milliken.

"I'm Tom Edison, and I've written to you for a job."

Milliken sized up the young man who stood in front of him. What a disreputable-looking hobo! His only protection against the cold was a long linen duster smudged all over with grease. His pants were too short and too tight. His shoes were torn and twisted out of shape. And his hair, which looked as if it hadn't been combed for a week, was topped by a hat with a wide brim. The hat was so ragged that one of Edison's ears stuck out through a hole. For a moment, Milliken was inclined to dismiss him. But then he held up Edison's application for the job and changed his mind.

"This is written in a beautiful script," he remarked. "Did you do it yourself?"

"Yes, sir."

"How did you get such a perfect handwriting? It looks almost like print."

"I developed it while taking down telegrams. I found it the quickest kind of script to write and the easiest to read."

"Very well," said Milliken, "come back at seven and I'll give you a trial."

Edison returned promptly at seven and found the clerks grinning at him. They had prepared an unpleasant surprise for him, arranging for the fastest operator in New York to send him a special news report of a thousand words. They would show up this country bumpkin who dared to apply for a telegrapher's job in a big city!

Edison sat down at a desk with a pile of blank sheets in front of him. "Ready!" he signaled, and the message began to pour in. Faster and faster came the words, but Edison's fingers flew over the blanks with equal speed. He happened to glance up for a moment, and then he understood the grins on the other men's faces. So they were trying to show him up, were they? Well, he would teach them a lesson!

Opening the key of his instrument, he tapped a message to the galloping operator in New York: "Come on, boy, don't go to sleep! Shake yourself and get busy with the other foot!"

The New York operator surrendered, and the clerks in the Boston office rushed up to him and slapped him on the back. They invited him to a restaurant and insisted on paying for his meal. Right then and there they acknowledged him as the "Speed King" of them all!

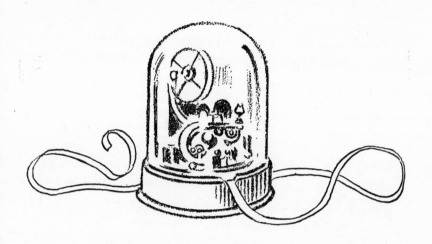

Chapter 5

THE LIGHTNING SLINGER

EDISON'S EXPERIMENTS, which had been more or less of a game in the past, were now beginning to take a practical turn. His chief aim was to discover things that would make life easier for other people. He had bought the works of the great British scientist, Michael Faraday, and he studied them at every possible opportunity. In order to widen the range of his studies he learned French and German, for many of the scientific books and articles written in these languages were not translated into English.

He was especially interested in electricity. The ease with which he had learned to handle this mysterious

force gave him the nickname of the "Lightning Slinger."
Once, when his fellow clerks complained of the roaches
that infested the office, he electrocuted the roaches with
a charged wire circuit, much to the amazement and de-
light of his friends.

But his principal concern at the moment was to invent a double telegraph transmitter—that is, an instrument that would send two messages over the same wire
at the same time. He remembered how he had once lost
his job for "fooling around with such crazy ideas." And
even now his superiors kept telling him that such an
invention was impossible. "Sending two opposite messages over the same wire is like sending two opposite
trains over the same track. There's bound to be a collision and a wreck."

But before long Edison turned his "impractical
dream" into an actual fact. He produced a double transmitter that really worked! He proved that two electrical
messages can bypass each other without any crash on
the way. Yet he was too poor to get out any patent on it.

At about the same time, he invented another interesting machine—an electrical contraption for the rapid
counting of votes in legislative bodies. He presented it
to a Congressional committee in Washington. The committee, however, turned it down. "If there is anything
on earth we don't want," said the chairman, "it is a
machine like this. We prefer to count our votes slowly,
for this gives us the time to persuade our colleagues to
change their minds when we think they are wrong."

Dissatisfied with his slow progress in Boston, Edison

decided to try his luck elsewhere. He took the night boat for New York and the next day arrived in the big city at dawn. His pocketbook was empty; he had spent his last cent on the ticket for the boat.

He slung his bag over his shoulder and walked up the street from the wharf. His hungry stomach was clamoring for food. Fortunately he passed a warehouse that had just received a load of tea from Ceylon. Through the window of the office he saw a man tasting samples of the newly arrived cargo. Boldly he walked into the office and asked for a cup of tea. "I can't pay for it, sir, but I shall be grateful for your kindness."

"Help yourself, young man, and welcome!"

This was Edison's first breakfast in New York. And his first lodging was in the cellar of the Gold Indicator Company. He received this temporary shelter through the help of an operator whom he had known while working for Western Union in Boston.

Here he stayed for a few nights, spending his days studying the company's instruments. The business of this company was to operate tickers that recorded the changes in the price of gold from hour to hour. This service was sold to several hundred customers who depended upon it constantly for their commercial activities.

But one afternoon, shortly after Edison's arrival in New York, the tickers broke down. There was panic at the offices of the Gold Indicator Company. Messenger boys rushed in from the various subscribers, screaming for service; engineers were racing from instrument to instrument in a vain effort to locate the trouble; and the president of the company, Mr. Samuel S. Laws, stood helplessly by, waiting for some miracle to happen.

And the miracle happened, in the person of Tom Edison. He walked up to the president. "I think I know what's the trouble," he said. "It looks as if a spring busted and fell down between two of the gear wheels."

"Then hurry up and fix it!" shouted Mr. Laws.

Tom had little trouble in locating the broken spring and resetting the contact wheels. Soon the entire ticker system was running as smoothly as ever.

Mr. Laws invited Edison into his office. "Would you like to work for us?" he asked.

"Yes, sir! I've been trying to see you about a job for several days. But they told me you were too busy."

"Well, from now on you're the foreman of the plant. And your salary is $300 a month."

"Thank you, sir!" cried Edison. And then he added in a bashful voice: "Would you mind advancing me a little money on my salary? I haven't had a square meal for several days."

Edison's new earnings seemed like a treasure out of the Arabian Nights. Yet they were nothing as compared to the windfall that awaited him at the very same office. A rival concern bought out the Gold Indicator Company. The name of this new business was the Gold and Stock Telegraph Company, whose president was General Marshall Lefferts. Edison was now working for a new boss who was looking for fresh and original ideas. This was a lucky thing for the young inventor. He had noticed that the stock ticker was an inferior instrument, and he suggested to General Lefferts that he might be able to invent something better.

"Go ahead and try," said the General.

Edison resigned his job as foreman of the Gold and Stock Telegraph Company, and opened a workshop of his own. He went into partnership with an electrical engineer, Franklin L. Pope. With the help of this man he worked on a new kind of stock ticker, and within a few months he finished it. He called it the Edison Universal Printer. This invention was simpler than the old instrument, and at the same time it was more effective. The spring and the gears were better adjusted and more securely fortified against breakdowns. And the various instruments in the system were so connected that all of them ticked off the same information at the same time.

Edison worked here on the same principle he had applied to his invention of duplex telegraphy. That is, he succeeded in multiplying the efficiency of his machine by getting the different parts to work together in a unit.

He took his new invention to General Lefferts. The General was enthusiastic and asked Edison how much he wanted for it. Edison remembered his unfortunate experience with the vote recorder. He mustn't expect too much for his inventions. What would be a reasonable price? Three thousand? Perhaps five thousand? And then he got an inspiration. "Suppose you make me an offer, General."

"Very well, would you accept forty thousand?"

Until he received his check, Edison was not sure whether General Lefferts had said *forty* thousand or *four* thousand. And even when he took the check to the bank, he suspected that he was the victim of a practical joke.

He felt sure of this when he presented the check to the paying teller. The teller returned it to him, saying: "You will have to endorse it, Mr. Edison." Because of his deafness, Tom was unable to make out the teller's words. Moreover, he knew nothing about endorsing checks—he had never handled any in the past. He therefore concluded that the "piece of paper" he had received from General Lefferts was no good.

So he snatched the check and rushed to the Gold and Stock Telegraph Company. General Lefferts had a good laugh over it. "All you had to do," he said, "was to sign your name on the back of the check." And then the General added: "I'll tell you what, Tom. My secretary will go along to identify you so that this time you'll have no trouble getting your cash."

When Tom returned to the bank, he asked for his money in small bills, for he was afraid that he wouldn't be able to change any bigger bills. He stuffed the greenbacks into his pockets, dashed home with his fabulous wealth, and stayed up all night to guard it against possible theft.

The next morning General Lefferts explained to him how to open a bank account and to take out whatever he needed from time to time.

And thus began a new period in the life of young Edison. He had arrived in New York hungry and penniless and with not a single job in sight. And now, only six months later, he was a budding capitalist with forty thousand dollars in the bank!

Edison was twenty-three. This is the age of fun and frolic in a young man's life, but Edison's mind was on other matters. He invested his time and his money in an up-to-date machine shop which he set up in Newark, New Jersey. He had received a big order for stock tickers from General Lefferts. He hired a number of men to manufacture the instruments and divided them into day and night shifts. Business was brisk, and his shop kept humming twenty-four hours a day.

He was his own foreman. He supervised the work of his mechanics and spent his spare time on experiments and new inventions. He averaged about four hours of sleep a day.

Within the next six years, from 1870 to 1876, the "lightning slinger" received patents for no less than 122 inventions. Yet these were only the shadows of the miracles he was to perform later on.

Chapter 6

THE WILL TO WORK

THE YEAR 1871, when Edison was twenty-four, brought him a tragic loss and a great happiness. The loss was the death of his mother, and the happiness was his marriage to Mary Stilwell. This is how it all happened:

When Edison's business had begun to prosper, he sent a letter to his parents telling them about his good luck. "You had better take it easy after this," he wrote. "Don't do any hard work, and get Mother anything she desires. You can draw on me for the money." And then he went on to tell them that he hoped before long to visit his mother, who had become an invalid. But before he got around to make the visit, his mother died. This was in April 1871.

For months Edison was broken up over his loss. He had adored his mother. "She was the making of me," he said, "so true, so sure of me, a constant blessing to me through the years."

But at last he got over the sharpness of his pain. He had found somebody else upon whom he could lavish his love. One rainy afternoon, the year before his mother's death, he had run out of his office for a bite of food. Two girls stood huddled in a doorway, trying to shield themselves from the downpour. He offered to help them to wherever they were going and they gratefully accepted his offer.

On the way he learned that they were sisters, Alice and Mary Stilwell. Both taught Sunday school. The more he talked to them, the more he fell under the spell of the younger sister, Mary. He asked if he might visit her, and she gave him a smiling "Yes."

Before long he began to wait for her at the Sunday school with a carriage, to take her home or for a drive into the country. And, in order to be near her as often as possible, he gave her a job in his laboratory.

One day, several months after his mother's death, he stopped at Mary's desk. Taking a silver coin out of his pocket, he tapped out a message in Morse code: "I love you very much. Will you be my wife?"

And Mary, taking the coin from his hand, tapped out in reply: "I love you, too. I will."

They were married on Christmas Day. Never particular about his clothes, Edison had quite an argument with his best man, who insisted upon Tom's wearing white gloves. He hated to "look like a dude." But finally he consented. "Anything for love," he said with a grin.

They had a brief honeymoon in Boston and then they returned to Newark and an eight-room house of their own. They wanted to have plenty of space for a growing family.

But he was too busy to enjoy the comforts of his home for any length of time. He was working on a new invention—the automatic telegraph. This instrument was designed to work without an operator at the receiving end. Instead, a metallic pen guided by an electric impulse was to write the messages on a chemically treated paper.

He had little difficulty in perfecting a pen that could send two hundred words a minute. But it was much harder to find the paper that could keep up with this speed. He decided to invent it himself. In order to learn all he could about the chemistry of paper, he ordered books from Paris, London and New York—enough to make a stack over five feet high. Then he settled down to study them.

Edison kept at it day and night for six weeks, eating at his desk and sleeping in his chair. And at last, after two thousand unsuccessful tests, he devised a carbon solution that resulted in the invention of paraffin paper. With this new paper he succeeded in recording not two hundred but thirty-one hundred words a minute.

But Edison was not satisfied with working on only one invention at a time. The subject of telegraphy had many angles that intrigued him. He had already discovered the principle of duplex telegraphy, and now he tried to expand the idea into multiplex telegraphy—the sending of four or more messages over a single wire. The principle, once he had discovered it, was simple. Just as you can send a stream of water in different amounts through pipes of different sizes, so can you send a stream of electricity in different currents through "condensers" of different powers of resistance. In this way you can divide the wire into several "pipes" or channels and use the different pipes for different messages at the same time.

In addition to his own inventions, Edison was called upon to straighten out the "bugs," or imperfections, in the inventions of other people. And thus he helped a man by the name of C. L. Sholes, who came to him from Milwaukee with a clumsy contraption he called a "typewriter."

When Edison examined it, he saw that the letters were not in alignment, the ink on the ribbon failed to flow properly, and the typewritten page presented a jumble of words that rose and dipped like the waves on a stormy sea.

Edison took it in hand, and within a few months he

produced the machine that has revolutionized the business of the world.

In the meantime his family was growing. About two years after their marriage, his wife gave birth to their first child, a beautiful little girl whom they called Marion Estelle. Three years later came their first boy; and, at the insistence of Mary, the father agreed to give him his own name—Thomas Alva Edison, Jr. But he gave the two children a couple of nicknames derived from Morse code—Dot and Dash.

And now there was another addition to his family. He had invited his father to come and live with him.

Sam Edison, though well advanced in years, was almost as agile as ever; and once again, as in his escape from Canada about forty years earlier, he demonstrated the power of his long legs. As he arrived at the New York City pier, suitcase in hand, to take the ferry for New Jersey, the boat was just pulling out. But this didn't stop the old man. Running back a little to get a start, he dashed to the edge of the pier, leaped across the water and landed on the retreating deck. The distance was estimated to be anywhere from ten to twenty feet.

He was surprised when the passengers on the ferryboat made a fuss over him. One of the passengers happened to be a reporter on the *New York Times*. "Would you mind giving me your name, sir?" he asked.

"Sam Edison."

"Do you happen to be related to the inventor?"

"I'm his father."

"Aren't you rather old for such a stunt?"

"Not at all, young man! I'm just a little over seventy."

The following day thousands of readers enjoyed the story about the old man's prowess. Like father like son, they said.

Shortly after Sam Edison's arrival in Newark, his son asked him to locate a quiet place in the country where a new research laboratory could be built.

"Why do you need a new laboratory, Tom?"

"I've outgrown the present shop. There are a lot of new inventions I want to work on."

"Haven't you already done enough inventing for one man?"

"No, Father, I haven't even begun."

Within a few days his father found a suitable spot. It was in Menlo Park, a beautiful New Jersey village of green valleys and low-lying hills situated about twenty-five miles from New York City. Here Edison set up his first big laboratory. Just a short distance from the laboratory he built a three-story home for his family. The spacious grounds contained a stable, a windmill, a big garden, and a wide lawn that served as a playground for his children.

Edison moved into his new laboratory in 1876. He was now, at the age of twenty-nine, an inventor with national fame. And before long he was to become world-famous as the "Wizard of Menlo Park." It was here that he was to unfold the miracles of several of his later inventions, including the phonograph, the electric light, the electric car, and the separate telephone receiver. Although the inventor of the telephone was

Alexander Graham Bell, it was Edison who gave the instrument a receiver as well as a transmitter, and who thus helped to develop it into the universal and handy telephone of today.

The development of the telephone—and the part that Edison played in it—makes one of the most interesting chapters in the story of modern science.

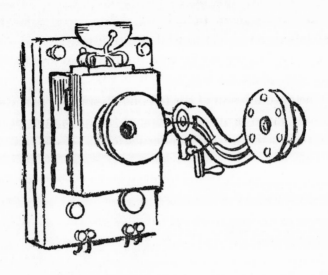

Chapter 7

FLYING VOICES

THE IDEA of the telephone came as a result of the successful use of the telegraph. If a wire could transmit metallic taps, why couldn't it transmit human speech? In other words, why couldn't a voice be made to fly through the air?

Bell and Edison were not alone in this idea. Another American, Elisha Gray, and a German, Philip Reis, were working on the same invention. And a race began among the four men for the building of the first telephone known to the civilized world.

The winner of the race was Bell. Gray was a close

second. He applied for a patent only a few hours after Bell had received one from the government.

But it remained for Edison to perfect the instrument. One day, while he was experimenting with air waves produced by different sounds, he discovered that the human voice could be transmitted over the air by a mouthpiece and received over the air by an earpiece.

This was quite an advance over Bell's invention, which required the users to speak and to listen through the same gadget. They had to shift it continually from mouth to ear and from ear to mouth in the course of a conversation.

Edison made one other important improvement in Bell's telephone. He strengthened the sound of the voice at the receiving end, and he got rid of the static which had made the messages on Bell's instrument very difficult to understand. Thus far, the public had regarded the telephone as little more than a clever toy. But with Edison's improvements the instrument began to look like an invention that could be put to practical use.

Edison took his improved telephone to William Orton, president of the Western Union Telegraph Company. "Mr. Orton," he said, "I have here a contrivance for which I believe there is a tremendous future."

And then he pointed out that Bell's telephone could be heard—and indistinctly at that—only over a distance of about twenty miles. But his own instrument, when first tested, gave a clear sound at more than a hundred miles. Orton offered him $100,000 for the rights to the transmitter. Edison accepted it on one condition:

"Please pay me at the rate of $6,000 a year. Otherwise I'd be tempted to spend the $100,000 all at once on my inventions."

Orton laughingly agreed. He knew that Edison was always ready to pour his money as well as his mind into his inventions.

While Edison was congratulating himself over his success with the transmitter, he received an offer for his receiver. This offer came from Samuel Insull, a young man who represented his interests in England. "Would thirty thousand be acceptable?" cabled Insull.

Edison, thinking that this meant thirty thousand dollars, accepted the offer. When he got the check, he was overjoyed to see that it was for thirty thousand pounds —a sum equal in those days to about a hundred and fifty thousand American dollars!

Money kept slipping through Edison's busy fingers. More experiments, more hired men to help him, and more materials to collect from every corner of the earth for his endless tests. Edison still kept steadily at work, even though at times he suffered from violent earaches as a result of his old injury. "I have seen him," said his sister-in-law, Alice Stilwell, "sitting on the edge of a bed and fairly grinding holes in the carpet with the heels of his shoes, he would be undergoing such pain."

But his hard work and his severe pain didn't keep him from playing with his children whenever he could find the time. "He was a great cut-up," continued Alice

Stilwell, "and he would put on Mary's dresses and romp about the house with the youngsters. They had a stereopticon and he would sometimes go behind the screen and stand on his head, and go through various antics to amuse them."

Edison would invite his friends to his laboratory to show them the wonder-world of his inventions. One night the Western Union Company gave a special telephone concert. The artists were in New York and the audience sat in Philadelphia, over ninety miles away. Edison's laboratory was connected by wires to both places, and his friends listened to the concert and marveled at the magician who had given wings to the music so that it could fly through the air.

This, we must remember, was several years before the invention of the radio. And even the radio might have been one of Edison's inventions had he not been so busy with his other work. Once, as he was leaning over his bench, he was surprised to see an electric spark speeding through the air between two carbon points. It was an exciting discovery, and Edison recorded it in his notebook: "This is simply wonderful and a good proof that the cause of the spark is a new and unknown force."

Edison had hit upon the secret of wireless telegraphy and radio, but at the moment his interest in the telephone was so strong that he made no further experiments with the free-flying spark. It remained for other men of genius—Marconi, Fleming and Baird—to develop this spark into a new form of miracle sound and miracle vision over the wireless air waves.

Chapter 8

THE MACHINE THAT COULD TALK
AND SING

EDISON spent on his inventions practically all
the money that he made—and all the time that he could
spare from his duties as a family man. He was perhaps
one of the most painstaking men that ever lived, and he
possessed a memory that was equal to his capacity for
work. When he looked at a machine, he could register
hundreds of details in his mind and recall every one of
them later on.

He needed his tireless patience and superb memory
for the jobs that lay ahead. The invention that mostly
absorbed him after his improvement of the telephone
was the phonograph. While working on his experiments in telegraphy, he had noticed that the tape which
recorded the messages would sometimes vibrate with

a musical sound. At the time he had filed away this observation in his retentive mind.

And now, in the summer of 1877, Edison was more or less free from other matters. One day he sat down at his desk and drew the sketch of a cylinder mounted on a long horizontal shaft. The left end of the shaft had a movable arm with a fingerlike needle at the tip. And the right end had a crank which turned the shaft along with the cylinder.

When the sketch was finished, Edison called John Kruesi, his laboratory foreman, into the office. "John," he said, "I want you to make this machine for me."

"I see nothing electrical in this machine, Mr. Edison. No coils, no magnets or wires. What is it good for?"

"It will talk and sing, John."

Kruesi shrugged his shoulders. His boss must be out of his mind. The result of overwork perhaps. But he went back to the shop and began to work on the machine. It was an easy contraption, and it didn't take him long to finish it. The cost of the material was eighteen dollars.

When he brought the machine back to the office, the bookkeeper was there with Edison.

"I'll bet a handful of cigars the machine can't sing or talk," said the bookkeeper.

"And I," said Kruesi, "will add two dollars to the bet."

"All right," replied Edison, "I'll take you on. I haven't any money with me, but I'll wager a barrel of apples."

He took the machine and asked for a sheet of tinfoil to wrap around the cylinder. When this was done, he turned the crank.

There was a loud scratch as the tinfoil began to tear. The bookkeeper winked at Kruesi, and Kruesi tapped his forehead. Both of them could already taste the cigars and the apples they would win at the boss's expense.

But Edison merely said: "Keep your shirt on, boys. I'm not through yet."

He asked for another piece of tinfoil and wrapped it more tightly around the cylinder, pasting the ends together to keep the tinfoil taut.

And then he turned the crank once more and slowly began to recite the childhood favorite, "Mary Had a Little Lamb." He went through the entire stanza, flipped back the mouthpiece, returned the cylinder to the starting position, and replaced the mouthpiece.

Suddenly the machine began to talk! It was Edison's voice, faint but distinct, that came back to them from the cylinder:

> Mary had a little lamb,
> Its fleece was white as snow . . .

Kruesi almost fell over in his fright; and even the bookkeeper, a far more courageous man, grew pale. "I'm happy to lose the bet," he stammered, "but this thing has me scared!"

"I'm a little scared myself," said Edison.

The next morning he took his new invention to the office of the *Scientific American*. The editor of this magazine, A. E. Beach, asked the inventor what that funny-looking object was good for.

"Just wait a moment," said Edison, "and you will find out." He placed the machine on Mr. Beach's desk. "Now turn the handle, if you please."

Beach did as he was told and looked as if he had just seen a ghost. For the lifeless machine was addressing him in a human voice! "Good morning, Mr. Beach, how do you like Mr. Edison's phonograph?"

"If this isn't a trick of ventriloquism," said Mr. Beach, "I'm looking at the greatest invention of the ages!"

And this "greatest invention of the ages" turned out to be the most sensational news of the day. Edison became the subject of many stories and cartoons in the papers. Some of the cartoons pictured him as a modern Merlin, wearing a black robe and a cap like an inverted ice-cream cone, and thrusting long bony fingers into the air as he tried to snatch the secrets of nature out of the sky. One Western magazine wrote that Edison was about to change all the laws of nature, causing water to run uphill, the earth to stop revolving on its axis, and the sun to shine at night!

Edison paid little attention to all this publicity. He was too busy straightening out his new machine. The voice was too scratchy, the tinfoil was unsatisfactory as a recording device, the cylinder had to be replaced with a flat disk, and many other defects had to be corrected before the phonograph could become a perfect instrument. It was to take him several years and three million dollars to complete the job to his own satisfaction.

But the public was too impatient to wait for perfection. Everybody wanted to see the talking and singing instrument as soon as possible. The members of Congress invited him to demonstrate it in Washington; and even the President, Rutherford B. Hayes, called upon him to bring it to the White House.

It was eleven o'clock at night when the summons from the President came to him at his Washington hotel. And it was four o'clock in the morning when Edison was allowed to go back to his hotel. As one of the guests at the White House remarked, "We have just spent a night of no sleep but amazing dreams."

Chapter 9

FROM SIMPLE SPEECH TO SYMPHONIES

SHORTLY AFTER THE invention of the phonograph, a reporter asked Edison what it was good for. And in a few words the inventor prophesied many of the things we know about the phonograph today. "It will be precious," he said, "as a family record. For it will preserve the sayings of those dear to us. It will keep alive the speeches of our great men, so that we may hear them after they are dead. It will take the place of books for the blind and the sick who are unable to read. And it will serve as a teacher for the mastery of new languages."

The phonograph, he predicted, would be a great favorite with the children. "It will enable them to hear nursery rhymes, to have dolls that speak, laugh and cry, imitation dogs that bark, cats that meow, lions that roar, and roosters that crow."

But the most important use of the phonograph, he declared, would be in the field of music. "Some day we shall hear full orchestras recorded upon this instrument, providing each of us with a front-row theater seat at home."

It was a long struggle for Edison to advance the phonograph to that point. He received a patent for his invention on February 19, 1898—the first patent ever granted for recording the human voice. And then he got busy improving the crude machine. He began a series of experiments on a disk that was to replace the cylinder. He tried all sorts of mineral fats and waxes to produce a record soft enough to receive a good impression yet hard enough to withstand wear and tear.

He found no satisfactory record that could be made out of this sort of material. And then he tried stearin, a substance derived from the animal fat in cow's milk. This gave him just the thing he was looking for—a strong, smooth surface that reproduced sound without a scratch. For many years this remained the chief material for the making of phonograph records.

After the experiments on the disk came a study of acoustics—the application of the laws of sound. Edison tried to discover the best ways of grouping singers or musical instruments in order to get the most beautiful results. He directed all this work himself; and, although partially deaf, he devised a special method of his own for hearing different sounds. "It takes a deaf man," he said, "to hear music. Most people hear only through their ears. I hear through my teeth and through my skull. Ordinarily I place my head against the phonograph. If there is some faint sound that I don't quite catch this way, I bite into the wood and I get it good and strong."

As Edison kept making improvements in his phonograph, he took out patents to protect his new ideas. Within ten years he secured about eighty such patents, each one marking another forward step toward the perfect machine.

And, as the machine kept getting better and better, he received more and more invitations to demonstrate it—in America, Europe, Africa and Asia.

One such invitation came from William II, the young Emperor of Germany. Edison was unable to accept the invitation himself; but he sent one of his representatives, A. T. E. Wangemann, to demonstrate the phonograph to the Emperor.

When Mr. Wangemann arrived at the palace, the Emperor called upon the court orchestra to make a record for the "strange music box." The members of the orchestra assembled in the concert hall, each one taking his accustomed seat. Mr. Wangemann explained that the record would sound better if the seats were rearranged so that some of the instruments could be brought nearer the phonograph while some of the others could be moved further away.

But the conductor was a temperamental gentleman. He refused to budge any of his players. Thus they had sat all the time, he insisted, and thus they would sit now.

At last the Emperor himself took a hand in the dispute. "By whose authority do you require the shifting of the players?" he asked Wangemann.

"By the authority of Mr. Edison, Your Majesty."

"Then the seats shall be rearranged. When Mr. Edison commands, even the Emperor must obey."

Thus the record was made as Edison had directed, and for the first time an orchestra playing in Europe was heard across the ocean in America. Edison's prophecy had come true. The phonograph had brought the music of the concert hall into the homes of all the people and had become a great source of happiness throughout the world.

When this was reported to Edison, he merely smiled and said: "I have still greater achievements in my mind. And I am working on them right now."

Chapter 10

LET THERE BE LIGHT!

EDISON had conceived a new idea—how to turn
night into day. For thousands of years the human race
had walked through the darkness, depending upon the
crudest materials such as pine knots, animal fats and
wax candles to light the way. And then there was a slight
improvement, when kerosene lamps and gaslights were
introduced.

But Edison was thinking of something still better.
Electric lighting. "If electricity can produce power
and heat," he said, "there is no reason why it couldn't

produce light. All that is needed is a substance that will burn properly under the stimulus of heat and power."

Edison was not alone in this thought. Other scientists were working upon the same idea. About forty years before Edison's birth a young Englishman, Humphry Davy, had produced a light by passing an electric current through two sticks of charcoal. Since the current formed an arch as it flickered over the curve between the two sticks, Davy named his invention "the arc light."

Other inventors adopted Davy's idea and tried to improve it. In 1876, a Russian by the name of Jablochoff made an arc lamp which he called "the electric candle." But it was no good for practical use. It burned glaringly for a little while and then went out. Several American scientists, including William Wallace, Moses G. Farmer and W. E. Sawyer, had produced arc lamps of their own. But these, too, were unsatisfactory. The inventors couldn't find a material that would be strong enough and burn long enough for practical use.

It took Edison to solve the puzzle. And the story of this solution is one of the great adventures of the human mind.

When he first began to work upon the problem, everybody told him that he was wasting his time. "It has been absolutely proved," wrote a New York editor, "that electric lighting is impossible. It is against the laws of Nature." But to Edison, the word "impossible" meant "possible if you work at it hard enough."

And so he set himself to the task. He organized an

"insomnia" squad—a group of assistants who were ready to sacrific their sleep whenever a special job had to be done in a hurry. It was a fortunate thing that he was deaf; it saved him from hearing himself dubbed as a "dreamer," a "boaster," and a "fool."

The first task to which this "foolish dreamer" set himself was to read every book and article he could find on the history and the science of lighting. He filled 200 notebooks, covering about 40,000 pages with observations and drawings. He learned that there is very little difference between heat and light. Even the cave men knew that they could make two sticks hot by rubbing them together, and that they could make them burn by rubbing them a little harder. Moreover, they knew that certain kinds of material burned brighter and longer than other kinds. This, then, was Edison's first task: He must find some material that would give a good light and at the same time resist the heat of the electricity that would tend to crumble it into ashes.

He selected several rare metals and spun them into fine threads. But none of them worked. They burned out too quickly.

Undismayed, Edison went on. For days, weeks and months he sat in his laboratory, trying metal after metal, thread after thread. And then a thought struck him. Perhaps he would get better results if he lighted his threads in a lamp, or bulb, that would be emptied of its air. He ordered a glass blower to make a number of pear-shaped bulbs, and then he pumped the air out of them.

The result was fair. When the oxygen was removed from the bulbs, the electrified threads burned brighter and longer. Edison had hit upon one of the important principles of electric lighting—the vacuum bulb.

But he was still dissatisfied. Even with his improved bulb, the light lasted only a few minutes. He had not yet discovered the right material for the filament, or burning thread. Somewhere in the world, he felt, this substance existed. But where? And how was it to be found?

This was a challenge that Edison met like a general planning a military campaign. He organized a group of scout technicians to wrest from nature the secret of the bright-burning and long-lasting filament.

At first they concentrated their efforts upon substances within reach of Menlo Park. They tried spools of thread, splinters of wood, tissue paper, silk, straw, cardboard, fish lines, hemp, rubber, cork, and even hairs from the beards of two of Edison's assistants. One of them had a curly black beard, and the other sported a beard of soft red hair. The black hair proved the more lasting under the electric heat. But this, together with all the other material they could lay their hands on, failed to fill the bill.

Edison and his assistants then tried dipping various filaments into black soot gathered from the chimneys of kerosene lamps. The lampblack hardened the filaments and gave out a better light. But the results were still far from satisfactory. One of the lights managed to survive over forty hours. Yet even this was not enough.

A year had gone by since the beginning of Edison's experiments on electric lighting. His eyes had become inflamed as a result of their exposure to the burning glare. He said nothing about this to his assistants or even to his wife. But he mentioned it in his notebook. "Suffered excruciating pains in my eyes last night from 10 P.M. till 4 A.M., when I got to sleep with a dose of morphine. Eyes getting better now, but I lose a day's work."

As soon as his eyes felt a little better, Edison went on with his work. And at last he was ready to show his invention to the world.

New Year's Eve, 1879. The inventor had invited hundreds of guests from New York and Philadelphia to come to a party at Menlo Park. It was night when the trains began to arrive. A light snow had fallen in the afternoon. As the train that carried the first visitors pulled into the station, Edison gave a signal to one of his engineers.

Suddenly the night disappeared and the blanket of snow that covered the countryside was transformed into a million diamonds under a flood of electric lights. Hundreds of lamps, like miniature suns, illumined the road that led from the station to the laboratory.

When the enchanted guests arrived at the laboratory, they found a number of mechanics dressed in their working clothes. "Where is Mr. Edison?" asked one of the visitors, expecting him, like themselves, to wear his best formal suit for the occasion.

"He's over there near the dynamo," said another visitor, a man who knew Edison by sight.

The inventor was examining the dynamo that converted mechanical power into electric light. He wore a gray flannel shirt, a pair of trousers stained with grease and chalk, and a coat in which the chemicals of the laboratory had burned a couple of holes. Edison was too busy for silk hats and full-dress suits.

But as soon as he was through with his examination of the dynamo, he greeted the visitors and entertained them with the story of the electric light. They hung upon his words hour after hour, as he took them from one machine to another, explaining their secrets and giving the proper credit to all the men who had helped him in his work.

As the evening wore on, there were a few incidents that startled and amused the visitors. Edison had put "Stay Out" warnings upon the doors of some of the rooms which contained the more powerful dynamos. Several of the guests who had failed to obey these signs found, to their amazement, that their watches were magnetized. And a young lady who strayed into one of the forbidden rooms rushed out with a terrified shriek, her hair standing up above her head. Her hairpins had popped out from her elegant hairdo when she came too close to a powerful generator.

Outside of these minor incidents, the party was a huge success. A number of his friends urged Edison to put his electric lamp on the market. But he was not yet ready for that. The filaments he had discovered thus far were still too fragile for practical use. Something stronger must be found!

One day he came across a bamboo fan in his laboratory. Taking it apart, he divided the cane into thin strips, covered them with lampblack, and inserted them in his bulbs. The results were very good.

Perhaps this was the secret he was looking for? He began to study up on the subject and learned that there were no less than twelve hundred different kinds of bamboo growing in various parts of the world. His mind was made up. He would send his "scouts" all over the world to find the best possible type of bamboo for making filaments.

It was a long and exhausting and expensive search. His men sent him more than six thousand samples of bamboo from every corner of the earth, and Edison tried them out in his laboratory one by one. Many of them ranged from "pretty good" to "good" to "very good." And then, one day, he got a specimen which he was able to mark "excellent." It was a bamboo that came from the jungles of the Amazon. The Edison electric lamp was ready for commercial use.

Chapter 11

CUPS OF ELECTRICITY

THE PROBLEM THAT now confronted Edison was how to pour a current of electricity into separate bulbs just as you pour a stream of water into separate cups. For this was the only way in which he would be able to supply thousands of homes with electric light.

Once again many people told him the thing was impossible. "In the first place," they said, "you can't divide electricity. In the second place, even if you could divide it, you couldn't measure the amounts used in the different homes. And in the third place, you could never produce an electric light that would be as cheap as a gaslight."

But Edison had undertaken to light the city of New York with electricity; and, to everybody's amazement but his own, he succeeded.

It was the most gigantic problem he had tackled thus far. He and his assistants had to build a central station, set up the machinery, dig up the streets of New York City, lay the wires, connect them in the different homes, and invent a meter for recording the various amounts used.

But, first of all, he had to raise the necessary funds for such an enormous enterprise. Fortunately he was a good salesman. He succeeded in interesting the famous banker, J. Pierpont Morgan, in his plans. Mr. Morgan organized the Edison Electric Company, with enough money to start and with a promise of more money to come if the work went along smoothly.

But there were times when the work did not go along smoothly, and Edison had to use all his powers of persuasion to keep his backers from backing out. He was grimly determined not to fail. The word *failure,* like the word *quit,* had never found a place in his vocabulary.

In order to be as close to his new job as possible, he moved to New York. It was twelve years after his first arrival in that city, penniless, hungry, and unknown. And now, at thirty-two, he was world-famous as the greatest inventor of the century.

He bought a four-story residence at 65 Fifth Avenue and converted it into an office building. And he invited

Samuel Insull, his brilliant representative in England, to become his private secretary. Then he opened several factories in nearby streets and set to work building the complicated machinery for generating and distributing the electricity for the city lights.

Edison had to start at the very bottom. "There is nothing that we can buy or that anybody else can make for us," he said to Charles Batchelor, one of his leading engineers. "We must build everything with our own hands."

He had hired two thousand men who were eager to lend a hand in his great undertaking. One of their first jobs was to install electric lighting in the *Columbia,* a steamship that sailed between New York and San Francisco. The insurance companies refused to insure the ship. They predicted that it would go up in flames before it reached its Western port. But the owner of the vessel, Henry Villard, had greater faith in Edison. And his faith was justified when the news of the *Columbia's* safe arrival in San Francisco was flashed round the world.

Edison, elated over his success, felt that another demonstration of the soundness of his ideas would do no harm. So he staged an electrical parade on Fifth Avenue. He got several hundred men to march down the avenue in a hollow square. Each of the men wore a helmet with a portable dynamo inside and an electric bulb on top. The leader of the parade, riding on a white horse, wielded a baton tipped with a similar bulb. At a signal from the leader, all the lamps lighted up. At another signal, the lights went out. The crowds were elated at this public performance by the "Wizard of Menlo Park." And even the doubters began to be a little doubtful about their doubts. Edison was able to turn to his more serious business with an easier mind.

He called this business of giving light to New York "the greatest adventure of my life." He felt a sense of deep responsibility toward the people who lived in the city. "For," as he said, "unknown things might happen on turning a mighty power loose under the streets and in the buildings of New York." Confident in his own ability, however, he took the chance.

Yet there was no smooth sailing for Edison even now. The Mayor of New York refused to give his permission for the laying of electric wires under the city streets. The gas companies, who provided most of the lighting for the city, put every obstacle in the way of the man who was "threatening to ruin their business." And even his bankers were becoming restless once more. The country had just gone through a long financial depression, from 1873 to 1879, and they were afraid of losing a million dollars or more on this "newfangled electric light."

But Edison's assurance was contagious. He convinced the Mayor and the bankers to go along with him and organized his crews for the job. Some of them began to dig the trenches for the underground cables. Others made a careful study of every home and office whose owners had agreed to change to electric lighting. Still others tried to figure out the daily cost of gaslight and

to see how they could lower this cost with electric lighting. The rest of the men busied themselves with the making of tubes and sockets, the laying of wires and the building of power engines. Some of these engines were made in a factory situated on a New Jersey hillside. They were so mighty and turned so rapidly—about 1,000 revolutions a minute—that they almost carried the entire hill away when the throttle was opened.

And the man who superintended every single item of the job was Edison himself. "I used to sleep nights on piles of pipes," he said, "and I attended to all the details on the job. There was nobody else who could do it."

One of the many things that nobody else could do was the inventing of the electric meter. But when Edison put his mind to a problem, he generally solved it. The meter that he invented consisted of a small glass cell containing a solution in which two zinc plates were immersed. As the electric current passed through the meter, it caused the zinc to move from one of the plates to the other. Since the amount of zinc that is moved by a current of a certain strength over a certain time remains always the same, it was easy to find out just how much current was used up in every home every month. The man who was hired to "read" the meter merely checked the plates from month to month.

And thus the lighting of New York was close to becoming a fact. Yet many people were still jittery about it—especially one day when the pavement became electrified and the horses began to dance in the street.

When this was reported to Edison, he rushed to the

troubled spot. He noticed that the surface of the street had become electrified through a leak in some of the underground conductors. The horses, as their hoofs touched the electrified places, received a slight shock which made them jump. It took Edison and his assistants several days to locate the defective conductors and to repair the damage.

But the people were still jittery. They were afraid that they might be electrocuted—either by the network of cables underground, or by the jungle of wires overhead. For there were about twenty miles of these cables and wires that crisscrossed one another throughout the lower section of New York.

As the work was nearing the day when the lights would be turned on, Edison himself became a little worried. Suppose the city blew up when all this current was let loose? It could happen! At that time, we must remember, electricity was as great a mystery as the hydrogen bomb is today. Nobody, not even Edison, knew how it would behave when set off on a large scale.

It was therefore with some misgiving that Edison gave the signal to pull the switch. The day was September 4, 1882. Edison was dressed in a frock coat and striped trousers, for it was a solemn occasion—the first time in history when a great city would be illuminated with the new light.

The switch was pulled, and the people of New York were greeted with a spectacle the like of which they had never seen before. The entire lower part of the city had become transformed into a gigantic Christmas tree festooned with thousands upon thousands of lamps.

And on this tree hung the promise of a gift for all mankind—a new golden age of healthier eyes through brighter light.

There was also a special gift for the men who had invested their money in this invention when almost everybody else had said it would be a complete failure. Every thousand dollars the bankers had put into the Edison Electric Company was now worth fifty thousand dollars.

When the reporters came to congratulate the inventor on his success, they found him back in his laboratory. He was once more dressed in his working clothes. They asked him to make a speech in a public hall. But Edison smilingly refused. "I have no time to speak about the inventions of yesterday," he said. "I must begin to think about the inventions of tomorrow. There is much yet to be done in the promotion of human happiness and comfort."

Chapter 12

WHEN THE LIGHT WENT OUT

ONCE A REPORTER asked Edison a peculiar question: "Mr. Edison, if you could have chosen your birthplace, where would you have preferred it to be?"

And Edison promptly replied: "The planet Mars."

"Do you mind telling me why?"

"Because the Martian day is forty minutes longer than ours."

Edison's working day was never long enough to satisfy him. His hands couldn't ever catch up with his mind. No sooner was he finished with one invention than several others were on the way. Now that electric lighting was an established fact, he turned to some of the other possible uses of electricity.

One day he was riding on a horsecar. It swayed from side to side as the horses dragged it wearily along the tracks. It was a slow and sickening process to get from place to place in a big city like New York.

And then an idea struck Edison. Why not use electricity to drive the street cars?

It was not a new idea. In 1834 Thomas Davenport, a Vermont blacksmith, had built a small circular track and a couple of cars that ran upon it with power supplied by an electric battery. At about the same time, a Scotsman named Robert Davidson had installed an electric motor in a car big enough to carry passengers.

But, as usual, what others had regarded as a mere toy became in the mind of Edison an idea that would benefit the world.

And again, as usual, the newspapers began to ridicule the idea. "If you want to pull a car," Edison read in one of the papers, "you must put an animal in front to pull it. Electric transportation is absolutely and utterly impracticable!"

Edison smiled at the article, and proceeded quietly to build his electric railway. And it was not long before the horsecars of the nation began to be replaced by electric cars.

The sight of the new electric cars, with their trolleys attached like broomsticks to wires in the air, inspired Oliver Wendell Holmes to make one of his interesting observations. "There are crowds of people," he said, "who ride through our streets on these new-fashioned cars with their witch-broomsticks overhead; and not more than one in a dozen among them thinks or cares a nickel's worth about the miracle that is wrought for their convenience. We ought to go down on our knees when one of these mighty caravans, car after car, spins by us, under the mystic impulse [of the inventor]."

Edison rarely limited himself to any one invention at a time. His mind was too rich and too full of ideas throughout his life. While he worked on some of his greatest inventions, he conducted experiments in various other fields. He tried to find all sorts of new ways to harness electricity for the service of mankind. He kept improving the telephone, the phonograph, and the transmission of multiple telegraphy—that is, the sending of several messages over the same wire. And he invented electric pens, addressing machines, a method for making plate glass, a formula for preserving food, and many other things.

Edison was not able to devote all his time to his inventions. There was a constant stream of lawsuits that kept him busy in the midst of his experiments. Other inventors felt that they were entitled to the credit and the money he received for some of his patents. And at times he believed that others were trying to deprive him of the fruits of his own hard labor. He had an especially long and uphill fight to prove his claim to the invention of the electric lamp. The patent he took out on the lamp gave him the right to it for seventeen years. But it took him fourteen years of court trials and decisions, and new trials and decisions, before he finally won his right. The patent had now only three more years to run.

Yet nothing ever stopped him. Whether he lost or won a trial, he went right ahead with his work. He had no time to brood over his defeats. Or to dwell upon his honors. When he received a medal for some extraordinary achievement, he would throw it into the pile of odds and ends that he labeled as his "useless junk." And when he could spare the time to attend a dinner in his honor, he was the least concerned among the guests. "I'm glad if anything I've done gives them a good time," he said.

He rarely made a speech in public. He allowed others to do the speaking for him. At one of the dinners held to celebrate "the birthday of the electric lamp," Thomas B. Connery, the managing editor of the New York *Herald,* told a story that showed how Edison practically "shook his inventions out of his sleeve." He recalled how the inventor had come into his office the day after the city's electric lights had been turned on for the first time. "Mr. Edison," continued Connery, "asked me how I liked the new lamps.

" 'Fine,' I said, 'except that I can't light my cigar with one of them.'

"Two days later, Mr. Edison came back to my office. 'Here,' he said, 'is something I've just invented for you.' And he handed me an electric cigar lighter."

This was Edison's simple, businesslike and efficient way of doing things. When the world needed a better system of communication, amusement, travel or light, Edison came and quietly said, "Here is something I've just invented for you."

But all his triumphs were forgotten when real tragedy struck. For several years his wife, Mary, had been in poor health. In the summer of 1884, she contracted typhoid fever. And, in spite of all the efforts of the best physicians, she died on August 9. They had been married for thirteen enchanted years.

For a time the light went out of his life along with Mary. But then he realized that he must not give in to his grief. He had his work to do, and his three young children—Marion, Thomas Alva Jr., and William—to care for. He sent his children to their grandmother Stilwell for the time being. She lived in New York and he was able to see them whenever he felt lonely in his big empty house. And he always came with presents for them—candy and toys for Tommy and Bill, and sheet music for Marion, who was taking lessons on the piano.

Sometimes he would take them on drives through Central Park. And occasionally he took Marion to a concert or to the opera, for both of them loved good music. In spite of his partial deafness, he could hear well enough to enjoy it and to point out the finer passages to Marion.

One day he told her about his experience at the performance of Gilbert and Sullivan's *Iolanthe* at the Bijou in Boston. He and Mary had attended in full evening dress, for it was a festive occasion—the first time an American theater was lighted by electricity.

"Suddenly," Edison told Marion, "I noticed that the electric lights were growing dim. I excused myself and hurried down to the power plant in the cellar. And what do you think I saw? The fireman who was supposed to be keeping up the steam to generate the electricity had fallen asleep.

"I threw off my coat, rolled up my sleeves, and began to shovel the coal into the dying flames. When the steam had got back to its original power, I cautioned the fireman to stay awake, put on my formal coat, and returned to my seat just in time to see the closing scene."

Edison forgot his loneliness when he spoke to his children about his life with their mother. But it was always with a heavy heart that he returned to his empty house.

Chapter 13

THE WORLD ON THE MARCH

EDISON was so busy with inventions that he soon found his old laboratories too small for his expanding thoughts. He decided to build a new plant in Schenectady, a picturesque little town on the Mohawk River in upstate New York. Shortly after the new plant was built, he organized a big corporation and began to manufacture all sorts of electrical equipment—from lamps and arc lights to street cars and locomotives.

But Edison devoted only a part of his time to his manufacturing interests. He turned the management of the plant over to competent supervisors and went back to his laboratory and his inventions. He felt that some of his greatest work still lay ahead.

And he was right. One May day in 1885, as he was

taking a holiday trip to Boston, he looked through the window of the speeding train and saw the landscape rushing by in the opposite direction. For a few minutes he was absorbed in the beauty of the scene as it danced in its spring drapery of leaves and flowers. And then a thought struck him: "This looks like a picture in motion."

His mind got immediately busy with the thought. Why not build a camera to reproduce this sort of moving picture? To show the world, not standing still as in the old pictures, but alive and on the march!

He decided to work on this idea as soon as he returned from his vacation. When he arrived in Boston, however, he forgot his moving pictures for a while. Something more interesting absorbed his mind. He was having dinner at the home of Ezra Gilliland, a friend from his old Western Union days. "There's a young lady I'd like you to meet," said Mrs. Gilliland. "Her name is Mina Miller. Her father is an inventor like yourself."

And Mrs. Gilliland went on to tell Edison that Mina Miller was educated and pretty and artistic and decidedly worth knowing.

"How old is she?" asked Edison. He wasn't much interested, but he wanted to be polite.

"She's just twenty."

Edison laughed. "Much too young for me. I'm thirty-eight, you know."

Mrs. Gilliland had a hard time persuading Edison to meet her friend. Edison protested that he wasn't the sort of person who could ever make a hit with a young girl. But Mrs. Gilliland persisted, and finally she had her way.

So the two met—and fell in love. They spent several weeks at Chautauqua, where the Miller family of six sons and five daughters had a summer home and a big boat. The parents welcomed Tom Edison as another son, and for almost the first time in his life the inventor learned to relax and have fun.

The couple became engaged in the fall; and during the Christmas holiday the Edison children for the first time met the "very pretty lady" who was to become their new mother. She appeared to them more like a sister, for she was only eight years older than Marion. She had come laden with gifts for the three children; before long, all four of them were chatting and romping together while the father looked on with a happy smile.

They were married two months later, on February 24, 1886. And they spent their honeymoon at Fort Myers, on the western coast of Florida, where the inventor had bought a big house with a spacious garden of palm trees, hibiscus, and flaming bougainvillea—a very Paradise for recreation and play.

Yet Edison's honeymoon was not entirely devoted to play. He had set up a laboratory in his villa, and he spent a good part of his vacation working among his wires and chemicals and bunsen burners and drill presses and lathes.

Time and again, as he toiled in this laboratory, his mind went back to his idea for making motion pictures.

He was determined to plunge into this venture seriously when he got back to his laboratory in the North.

On his return from his honeymoon, he presented his bride with a house in Llewellyn Park, at the foot of the Orange Mountains. It was one of the showplaces of New Jersey—a house of red brick nestled in a thirteen-acre park of flowers and trees and velvet-green lawns. Here he brought his three children and settled down to a new life that was to bring him continual happiness for more than forty years.

For to Edison, happiness meant a loving family, an understanding wife, hard work, good music, and a chance to putter around in his garden. He cared little for the games and sports of other people. He detested bridge and poker. And he considered golf a useless pastime. He thought it much more fun to walk with his arms swinging free instead of being burdened with a golf club having to stop again and again in order to hit a ball.

His favorite amusement was listening to his wife as she sat at the piano. He would puff on his cigar, shut his eyes, and dream about the time he would make a record perfect enough to play a whole symphony of Beethoven's, and a picture vivid enough to show the entire world on the march.

He meant to bring a concert hall and a theater into every home. He wanted everybody to hear the best music on his own record, and to see the best plays and parades on his own screen.

His main interest now was his motion-picture idea. He worked on this idea, off and on, for several years. But, as usual, this was not the only project that occupied his time. To keep up with his business interests and his inventions, he built a new laboratory at West Orange, New Jersey. This laboratory, the largest in the world, was only half a mile from his home. And thus he managed to spend more time with his family.

He rarely returned home from the laboratory empty-handed. He brought "trick" alarm clocks to the children and taught the boys how to take them apart and put them together again. Once he came home with a tiny steam engine that was run by an alcohol flame. And time and again he contrived other toy inventions and gadgets for the amusement of the children.

Before many years, the number of his children had grown to six—one girl and two boys by his second marriage added to the one girl and the two boys by his first marriage. Two daughters and four sons. He frequently took his children to the laboratory at West Orange, and he fixed up for them a little workroom of their own.

One day there was an explosion in the children's laboratory. The boys had tried to invent a "floating bomb" which burst into pieces, shattered the window and nearly killed one of them. From that day on, Edison insisted upon guiding them himself through all their experiments.

It was a joyous and affectionate family life at Llewellyn Park—especially at Christmas after the presents had been distributed, when they would gather around the piano and enjoy a holiday songfest to the accompaniment of Mina's playing.

But always, after his short periods of fun, Edison plunged back to his work. And he was so absorbed in his work that he frequently sank into spells of absentmindedness. One day, when he went to register his latest invention at the patent office in Washington, he became so lost in his thoughts that he was unable to remember his name. On another occasion his absentmindedness resulted in an amusing incident at the laboratory.

Tired after a long stretch of work, he decided to lie down for a nap. He asked one of his assistants, Charlie Batchelor, to bring him his lunch at two o'clock. The assistant came back at the appointed time, placed the lunch on a table, and awakened the inventor. Edison opened his eyes, glanced at the food, and promptly fell asleep again.

This gave Batchelor an idea. He ate the boss's lunch himself and replaced the tray with the leftovers on the laboratory table.

A few minutes later Edison awoke again. Seeing the remainders of the lunch, he concluded that he had eaten his meal. He pulled out his after-dinner cigar from his pocket and began to puff away.

Just then Batchelor returned. "How did you enjoy your lunch, Mr. Edison?" he asked, with a mischievous grin.

"All right, I guess. But I still feel a bit hungry."

"No wonder, Mr. Edison. It was I who ate your lunch!"

Edison glared at his assistant, but a hearty substitute meal quickly restored his good nature. "Hereafter," he laughed, "I shall have to watch out, or you rascals will be the end of me and my problems!"

Among the chief problems that occupied Edison at this time were the moving-picture machine and an exhibit of his inventions at the Paris Centennial Exposition (in 1889). At the insistence of Mrs. Edison, he decided that they would take a holiday and attend the

Exposition in person. Marion Edison, now a charming young lady of sixteen, went along with them.

The Edison inventions took up one third of the entire space devoted to American exhibits. And the principal sensations of these exhibits were the new phonographs and the enormous electric lamp forty feet high resting upon a pedestal twenty feet square.

But even more sensational than these inventions was the presence of the inventor himself. The crowds forgot the royal visitors from all over the world and flocked to see the modest American with his good-natured smile. The city officials of Paris gave a banquet in his honor, and 9,000 guests came to pay him tribute. They stood up and burst into applause when he walked into the dining hall with Mina and Marion, "the two most beautiful women in the world," on his arms.

At the end of the dinner there were speeches in honor of "the genius of the age" and a piano recital by Gounod, the creator of the opera *Faust*. He now played a composition which he had written especially for the occasion, and he presented an autographed copy of the piece to the Edisons.

The closing event of the evening was the decoration of the inventor as a Commander of the Legion of Honor. The medal that indicated this honor was pinned upon the lapel of Edison's coat by the French President, Carnot.

But when the President wasn't looking, Edison unpinned the medal and slipped it into his pocket.

From Paris, the Edisons traveled to Berlin, London,

and Rome. In the Italian capital Mr. and Mrs. Edison became, at the command of King Humbert, the Count and the Countess Edison.

But when he left Rome Edison placed the insignia of his Italian nobility in his pocket, too. He returned to America as plain Tom Edison, whose only claim to aristocracy was an active mind and a willingness to work.

And now that the vacation with all its excitement was behind him, Edison returned to his laboratory and threw himself heart and soul into the work he had been planning for a long time—the creation of the moving-picture machine.

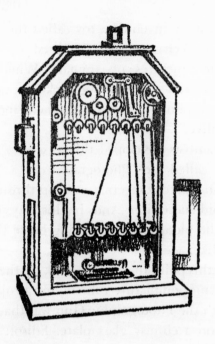

Chapter 14

LIVING PICTURES

LIKE MANY of his other inventions, the idea of pictures in motion did not originate with Edison. For thousands of years, poets and scientists had been talking about "images that appear to move." They had seen the shadows of clouds speeding under the sun, and they had hinted at some sort of machine that could reproduce this shadow motion later on.

It was not till 1860, however, that a man by the name

of W. H. Horner invented a toy called the "Wheel of Life." This mechanical toy consisted of a cylinder covered with pictures of animals. When someone whirled the cylinder around and looked at the pictures through a peephole, he could see them moving as if they were alive.

Other scientists developed this idea into a machine which they called the "Photographic Gun." This machine, or camera, took several snapshots through a single lens in rapid succession. And, in this way, the viewer could see the picture of a galloping horse that looked almost lifelike.

It was at this point that Edison took up the search for the perfect motion-picture camera and projector. The trouble with the Photographic Gun was that it took its exposures on a clumsy glass plate. Edison wanted to find something that was less bulky—a sort of flexible tape, or film, that could be rolled around a spool and then rapidly unrolled as the pictures were taken.

He went with his problem to George Eastman, the famous manufacturer of photographic materials. And together the two inventors set to work experimenting on films that might replace the bulky plates.

But Edison had to start from the beginning. He had never taken a picture or even handled a camera in his life. His first job, therefore, was to become an expert in the history and the science of photography. With the help of Eastman and all the books and articles he could find on the subject, he soon got to know more about photography than any other living man. This was al-

ways the way with Edison. He *accomplished* more because he *knew* more.

Yet with all his knowledge, it took him a long time
and many experiments to discover the right material
for the films. At first he tried thin paper covered with
a gelatin emulsion. But the paper tore too easily. And
then, after thousands of trials and errors, he hit upon
celluloid as a means for strengthening the films. As
soon as this new material was tried, Edison knew that
this part of the problem was solved. "We've got it,
boys!" he cried. "Now we must really get to work!"

And he worked persistently until he was ready to
give to the world a machine which, in his own words,
"will do for the eye what the phonograph does for the
ear." He called his new machine the "Kinetoscope"—
or the reflector of motion in pictures. He had great
hopes for this moving-picture machine. "The time is
coming," he said, "when the moving picture and the
phonograph will be combined so naturally that we shall
be able to produce grand opera on the screen. And the
result will be so realistic that the critics themselves will
be deceived."

As everybody now knows, Edison's dream has been
fully realized. Yet the first pictures taken by his kinetoscope were extremely crude. In their effort to find interesting material for the amusement of the public,
Edison and his assistants used up miles of film on all
sorts of movements and stunts. One of the mechanics at
the laboratory, whose name was Fred Ott, was famous
for a sneeze "that sounded like a thunderbolt." Among

the first pictures to be reproduced on the camera was this sneeze, in all its amusing contortions, photographed at the rate of fifty pictures a second. Some of the other earliest pictures represented the mechanics in the act of turning somersaults, standing on their heads, and indulging in all sorts of funny faces and crazy antics.

A "special feature" of the early photographs was a training bout between the champion prize fighter, John L. Sullivan, and an unknown pugilist who had been hired for the occasion. But this picture never came out as intended. As soon as the hired boxer recognized the "champ," he turned on his heels and rushed out of the studio as the cameras clicked away.

Everybody in the laboratory took a turn at acting for the camera—except one man. The sole exception was Edison himself. "My job is not to show off," he said, "but to work."

Among the "trick" pictures taken at this time was the "accident" suffered by an artist busy at his canvas on a railroad track. Suddenly an express thundered into the picture, scattering artist, canvas and easel in a thousand pieces all over the scene. But as soon as the train passed, the pieces gathered themselves together again; and the artist, after shaking his fist at the interruption, went on with his painting in the middle of the track.

The world's first moving-picture studio was built in a yard near Edison's laboratory at West Orange. It was an oblong building set to revolve on a circular track, so as to catch the sun at all times of the day. It resembled a huge camera and it was painted black on the inside. Edison called it the "Black Maria."

And the earliest public view of motion pictures was not through the modern screen but through a "Peephole Machine"—a boxlike contraption fitted with a glass window slit that enabled the spectator to look inside. Only one person at a time could see the picture through the narrow slit. It was first exhibited at the Chicago Fair, and it carried thousands of visitors into a new and magic world.

Edison was dissatisfied with this contrivance. He wanted thousands of people to see the pictures at the same time. So he invented a projecting machine and constructed a screen upon which the pictures were to be enlarged. "The projecting machine," he explained, "is nothing but the camera in reverse." The camera reduces a big object to a small picture, and the projector magnifies the small picture to the original size of the object.

It seems simple enough to our own generation, but to the people in Edison's day it was one of the marvels of the century. The first New York projection of a motion picture on a screen took place on April 27, 1896. The audience was wild with enthusiasm. "This sort of thing," said a reporter, "will enable the future to see the past—how people lived, crowned and buried their kings, drilled their armies, launched their battleships, played their games, worshipped in their churches and taught in their schools."

One of the greatest triumphs of Edison's new invention was in the field of nature. The camera recorded the growth of a flower over a period of several weeks, and then reproduced it upon a screen in the space of a few minutes. And thus the development of a simple plant, from seed to bud, from bud to petal, and from petal to full-grown flower open to receive the rain and the sun, was displayed for the first time in its entirety.

When Edison was through with the invention of his moving-picture machinery, he turned over to others the commercial and artistic development of the "silver screen." He explained that he was a mechanic, not a showman. He sold his patent to a company which was to grow into one of the richest business enterprises in the world. But he cautioned the new owners of his patent to use it for the benefit of mankind. "I believe that you control the most powerful instrument for good and evil," he told them. "Remember that you are the servants of the public, and never let a desire for money or power prevent you from giving to the public the best work of which you are capable. It is not the quantity of riches that counts; it's the quality which produces happiness."

And thus Edison disposed of his rights in the motion picture industry, and went back to his workshop with his head full of new inventions and new dreams.

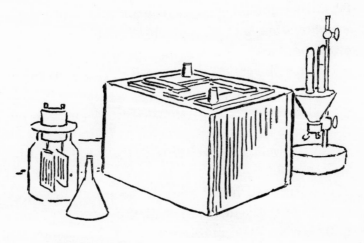

Chapter 15

TO MAKE LIFE BETTER FOR ALL

EDISON was now at work on three new projects
—the invention of the storage battery, the grinding of
mountains into metal, and the manufacture of cement
for the building of houses.

The inventor had been busy with his electric storage
battery for some time when he first met Henry Ford.
It was at a convention of engineers and officers of the
Edison Electric Company. The date was August 12,
1896; the place, the banquet room of the Oriental
Hotel at Manhattan Beach, near Coney Island, New
York. At the head of the table sat Edison himself.

The guests were conversing about the news of the
day—the race between Bryan and McKinley for the

Presidency, the plight of the Cubans under their Spanish oppressors, and the growth of American industry throughout the world. And then the talk drifted to some of the latest inventions that helped to enrich American business. One of the dinner guests asked Edison how he was getting along with his storage battery for street cars and electric trains.

"Pretty well," replied Edison, "but it is far from perfect as yet."

The guest touched Edison on the arm. "Do you see that young fellow across the table?"

"Yes, what about him?"

"He has just invented a machine that could use your batteries."

Edison was interested. "What sort of machine is it?"

"A gasoline car that moves by itself, without a horse."

"Really? Sounds very good." And, turning to Henry Ford, he said: "Young man, do you mind telling me about that invention of yours?"

The man who sat next to Edison got up from his chair and offered it to Ford. The young inventor, flushed with the excitement of meeting "the greatest genius of the day," took the empty seat and began to explain his idea of the automobile. He told Edison that the machine was a four-cycle engine and that he was now working on a spark plug that would explode the gas vapors in the cylinders; thus the gasoline would be transformed into power for driving the car.

As Ford went on with his explanation, Edison became more and more interested. Finally his fist came down upon the table with a bang. "Young man," he exclaimed, "that's the thing! You've got it! Electric cars must keep close to power stations. The storage battery that this requires is too heavy. Steam cars won't do, either, for they have to have a boiler fire. But your car is self-contained. It carries its own power plant—no fire, no boiler, no smoke and no steam. You've got the right idea. Keep at it!"

This was the beginning of a lifelong friendship between the two inventors. And the exchange of their ideas gave Edison an additional spur to his work on a more efficient battery.

The batteries in use at the time were too heavy to handle and too easily broken. Edison's job was to make a battery that was not only lighter but also stronger. In his effort to make this "dream battery," the inventor performed no less than fifty thousand experiments. Failure after failure after failure, but Edison went on.

It took the inventor ten years to find his perfect battery. Again and again the papers reported that "the Edison battery was a failure." But Edison never lost faith in his final victory. "If we search long enough," he declared, "nature will not refuse to yield up her secret."

At one time his battery was *nearly* perfect. Out of five thousand that he made, only two hundred were unsatisfactory. Everybody told him to stop. "Your product is good enough for the market, so why waste any more time on it?"

Why? Because the product wasn't good enough for Edison. His motto was: "Either perfection or nothing."

So he kept on improving his batteries, testing them on all sorts of roads and in all kinds of weather. When a road was particularly bumpy, Edison selected the roughest part of it for a number of special tests. Some of the cars that carried the batteries were wrecked, the tires wore out and the axles broke, but the batteries held up. Yet even this sort of trial was not enough. When a battery returned from its road test, it was exposed to a severe pounding in the laboratory.

Finally Edison succeeded in building a battery which was able to stand the road and laboratory tests without the slightest break. "I now believe," said the inventor, "that the problem of automobile traffic has been solved."

Edison thus helped to bring Ford's motor car, as he had helped to bring Bell's telephone, into practical use. Other inventors, too, came to him for assistance. One day, as mentioned earlier in this book, Edison had noticed a strange thing in his laboratory—an electric spark jumping through the empty air between two wires. He had made a note of it in his notebook: "This is simply wonderful and a good proof that the cause of the spark is a new and unknown force."

Though Edison did not realize it at the time, he had just hit upon the secret of wireless telegraphy, radio and television. He was too busy just then to experiment with this mysterious force that traveled over the air waves. But he took out some patents on his discovery, with the thought that he might work on it at some future date.

And now, years later, while he was working on his storage battery, he received a visit from Guglielmo Marconi. This young Italian inventor had just astonished the world by sending a message across the Atlantic without wires. He came to ask Edison's permission for the use of his patents; and Edison was eager to befriend Marconi just as he befriended Henry Ford. He gave not only his patents but his fatherly advice to his youthful visitor. "I have been watching your work for some time," he said, "and I admire your persistence in the face of public ridicule and repeated failure. Keep it up. You're a man after my own heart."

Edison was always intent upon helping others. His main business was to make the world a happier and less expensive place to live in. Easier communication, better lighting, the finest music in every home, speedier travel, and the world in motion on the silver screen—these were just a few of Edison's gifts to mankind. Whenever he thought of a new invention, he asked himself, "What good will it do for the world?"

This was the thought that occupied his mind one day during a vacation at the seashore, when he noticed a patch of black sand on the beach. He filled his pockets with the sand and took it back to the laboratory. As he was pouring it out on a table, a workman stumbled against it and dropped a big magnet he was carrying. The magnet fell on the sand.

When the workman picked up the magnet, Edison noticed that it was covered with tiny black grains. "This sand," said Edison, "must contain some sort of metal that is attracted by the magnet."

Immediately the inventor was plunged into deep thought. Out of this thought came the experiments that resulted in his invention of the magnetic ore separator. By means of this separator, he was able to extract thousands of tons of iron from the ore-bearing rocks of New Jersey.

The process was simple. He built a huge pincerlike machine that caught up a rock between its jaws and crushed it like a lump of sugar. And then, with the help of an electromagnet, he attracted the iron particles and separated them from the rest of the pile.

He built a plant for his new enterprise, and set up a town called Edison for the workers. He had visions of grinding entire mountains into dust, and of extracting from the dust enough iron to supply the world for many years to come.

But the project failed—and not because of any error on Edison's part. Just as the business began to prosper, another company discovered a rich deposit of iron in the mountains of Minnesota. And the cost of mining this iron was so much less than that of the Edison method that he had to abandon his venture on the very verge of success.

Edison took his failures, like his triumphs, in even stride. After every invention, whether it was successful or not, he asked himself, "What next?"

His next project was to find a new kind of material for the building of houses at a low cost. "My desire,"

he said, "has always been to create the largest possible
prosperity for the greatest possible number of people.
I think we can help do this by producing a better
cement at a lower price. Before we get through, we shall
be able to build a six-room house of cement for as little
as $300."

Edison decided to construct his new success out of his
previous failure. He planned to transform his iron-
extracting crushers into cement-making machines. And
so he went to his abandoned factory at Edison on a
Saturday morning, and spent several hours studying
the plant and figuring out ways and means of making
the necessary change. He examined every part of every
machine, but took no notes on paper. He just recorded
everything in his memory.

When he returned home, he had his supper and then
sat down at his desk. He stayed there all night and the
next morning, working out his ideas for the cement
factory. When he was through, he had written down
about six hundred items he had observed at the iron-ore
factory.

Then he built a factory that cost him $100,000 and
produced an entire house, including stairways, bath-
tubs, laundry tubs, window frames, mantels and pic-
ture-moldings, all of concrete. He superintended most
of the work himself, often at great risk to life and limb.
Once, when he was directing the grinding of rocks into
cement dust, he was caught in a landslide from which
he barely escaped. At another time, a steel spring from a
crusher broke loose and went hurtling through the air.

It barely missed Edison's nose and cut clear through a plank two inches thick.

But Edison persisted in his work and smiled at his dangers, until at last the workingman's "dream house" was complete.

Edison never got around to manufacturing this concrete house on a large scale. He left the project to men who were interested in the real-estate business. When they took up the Edison process, however, they dropped the idea of low-cost houses for everybody. Instead, they used his cement mostly for the more profitable construction of office buildings, bridges, factories, and baseball parks like the Yankee Stadium in New York City.

And thus another of Edison's inventions was put to practical use, but not in the way he had hoped. Edison was interested not so much in greater riches for the few, but in greater comfort for all. He was never too busy with his machines to forget his love for mankind.

Chapter 16

IN THE SERVICE OF HIS COUNTRY

ON JUNE 28, 1914, a young Serbian student assassinated Archduke Francis Ferdinand of Austria. This act of violence, committed at Sarajevo, an obscure little city in Bosnia, interrupted the work of the entire world —including Edison's. Europe was plunged into war, Germany was blockaded by the British Navy, America suffered from a shortage of important chemicals that had come from Germany, and Edison was called to the rescue.

Edison hated war. He refused to invent anything that would kill men. "I would rather make people laugh," he said. But he did agree to help with the supply of defensive chemicals, things that would save lives and keep business going.

One of the chemicals that America especially needed was carbolic acid. A shortage of this chemical, used as an antiseptic in the treatment of wounds, was a serious matter. In addition to that, Edison had a personal interest in carbolic acid. His formula for making disk records required a ton and a half of this chemical every day.

But it could be produced only out of a certain kind of coal, and Germany was the only country which had a big enough supply of this coal for the purpose. Something had to be done to produce this chemical in the United States. And Edison found the way.

"If we can't make carbolic acid out of coal," he said, "we can make it out of something else."

"But how?" asked one of his engineers.

"Synthetically—that is, by combining other chemicals that would give us the same results we would get out of coal."

Again the word "impossible" was flung into his face.

"Don't call anything impossible," said Edison, "until you try."

So once more Edison set out to do what everybody told him couldn't be done. He had to work fast, because the shortage in carbolic acid was becoming critical. He organized a squad who worked in shifts twenty-four hours a day. In less than a week they had the plans ready for the construction of a new factory. Edison asked some of his manufacturing friends how long it would take them to build the plant and deliver the goods.

"But we don't know how to go about it," they said.

"I'll show you how."

"Well, in that case it would take nine months—perhaps six if we're very lucky. But certainly not less than six months."

"We can't wait that long," exclaimed Edison. "Our shortage is right now!"

"What are you going to do?" asked one of the manufacturers.

"I'll build the plant myself."

He mobilized his workers and set them an example of almost superhuman will. Inspired by his determination and drive, they finished the factory—not in nine months or in six months, but in *seventeen days*. On the eighteenth day the plant produced seven hundred pounds of synthetic carbolic acid. Within a month, the plant was able to turn out a ton a day.

Throughout his life, Edison had trained himself to build victory out of defeat. Now, in the midst of his latest victory, another defeat stared him in the face. A fire had destroyed six of the buildings in his West Orange plant. It was on the night of December 9, 1914. The loss was about five million dollars, and the buildings were not insured. "This," thought his friends, "is the end."

But Edison thought otherwise. Among the ruins of the fire he had found a photograph of himself. The frame was charred and the glass was cracked, but the smiling face of the inventor remained unscathed. As Edison looked at the likeness of himself that had been rescued from the flames, he smilingly observed, "Never touched me!"

The inventor, at sixty-seven, was ready to begin all over again. "No one," he said, "is ever too old to make a fresh start." The day after the fire he was ready with the drawings for the rebuilding of the plant.

Edison had neither the time nor the desire to lament his personal loss. The country needed his services. In addition to the shortage in carbolic acid, there was a scarcity of several other chemicals that had been imported from Germany. Some of these chemicals were prepared in a secret manner known only to the Germans. Among them was a formula used in the dyeing of furs. When the dye stopped coming to America, the furriers went to Edison for help. Realizing that thousands of laborers would lose their jobs if the fur industry failed, the "Wizard" prepared a new formula and began to make the dyes in one of his own factories.

As the war progressed, Edison's services came to be more and more in demand. But he always insisted upon helping to save rather than to kill people. When the Germans sank the *Lusitania,* on May 7, 1915, and the seas became unsafe for American travel, the government drafted Edison to head a group of scientists who would help in the emergency. These and other civilians who gave all their time to the service of their country were called "dollar-a-year" men, since a dollar a year was the entire pay they received for their sacrifice.

He became the head of the Naval Consulting Board; and when he appeared in public, he was accompanied by Secret Service men to protect him. For he had received letters threatening that he and his laboratory would be "blown up to heaven" if he continued to work against the interests of the German Kaiser.

Edison, however, refused to be stopped by danger just as he had refused to be stopped by ridicule. He worked persistently throughout the war; and, at an age when most people are happy to retire from work, he produced more than forty inventions for saving property and life.

Let us glance at just a few of his wartime inventions:

An apparatus that enabled a ship to hear the sound of a torpedo as it was fired from a submarine more than two miles away, and a method to change the ship's course in a hurry so that the torpedo would miss the mark.

Collision-repair mats to plug the holes made by torpedoes that succeeded in striking the ships. These mats were so arranged that they could be placed into position to cover the rents within fifteen seconds after the torpedoes had struck.

A system of camouflage that discolored the water around a ship and thus saved the ship from being observed by an attacking submarine.

Special night lights for ships traveling together in a convoy. These lights were visible to other ships in the convoy but were hidden from enemy submarines by a combination of black disks that threw the beams horizontally across the sea but not vertically down into the depths.

A system of detecting cables that enabled submarine chasers to guide merchant ships out of mined harbors. Two chasers, steaming in parallel lines across the harbor, had an underwater cable suspended between them. As the cable swept the harbor, the merchant ship followed about half a mile behind. Whenever the cable encountered a mine, the chasers warned the ship to change its course.

Among his other wartime inventions were devices for locating hidden guns, gas masks, finders for detecting enemy airplanes, a system of searchlights which sent telegrams in Morse code from ship to ship, and a method for preserving underwater machinery from rust. The story of Edison's military inventions has never been completely told, for some of them are military secrets. But, as a result of his contribution to our national defense, he won the Distinguished Service Medal. No other civilian in the Navy Department received this award.

Edison was happy to get the distinction. But he was even happier to see the end of the slaughter. On Armistice Day, November 11, 1918, he laid down his military burden and went back to his peaceful work.

He was now seventy-two. One of his friends advised him to rest. "You are growing old, you know."

"Growing old?" retorted Edison. "Look!"

He extended his right arm and bent over until the

fingers touched the tip of one of his shoes. Then he spun around on the other foot like a top.

"How do you manage to do it?" asked his astonished friend.

"By watching my diet. I eat three meals a day, but very little at each meal. Enough to nourish my body, but not enough to make me food-drunk."

"And what about exercise?"

"My regular work gives me all the exercise I need."

And then he added as an afterthought: "I have to keep my body in shape, you know. It's the most important piece of machinery I have. It carries my brain around."

Chapter 17

"INTERESTED IN EVERYTHING"

AT SEVENTY-FOUR, Edison's body was still strong enough to carry his amazing brain. But he reduced his working schedule from sixteen to fourteen hours a day. He wanted to spend a little more time at home with his family. The greatest thing in his life, greater even than the triumph of his inventions, was his love for Mina. He never left his house, even if for an hour or so, without kissing her and telling her where he was going.

Mina returned his love in full measure. She brushed his clothes for him, gently scolded him when his tie was not on straight, and read to him the stories he loved best. He was especially fond of mystery stories. "My whole life," he said, "has been a search into the mysteries of nature."

In spite of his deafness, he could hear Mina perfectly when she read or spoke to him. "I can read her lips, her eyes, her heart."

Edison spent his seventy-fifth birthday by going to work, as usual, in his laboratory. When the reporters came to interview him, he stepped outside and stood bareheaded in the rain so that they could take several snapshots of him.

"When do you expect to retire?" asked one of the reporters.

"Never."

"What are you especially interested in?"

"Everything."

"To what do you attribute your genius?"

"There's no such thing in the world," retorted Edison. "What some people choose to call my genius is just plain hard work—ninety-eight per cent perspiration and two per cent inspiration."

When he was asked how rich he had become through his inventions, he replied: "I have made a lot of money, it is true. But money has a habit of getting away from me because I am always experimenting, and that costs a heap."

Always experimenting. At eighty he devised a "long-playing" phonograph which was able to play forty minutes of music on a single record. The new record was no bigger than the old; but the length of the composition it reproduced, if recorded in the old manner, would have taken a disk almost as big as a dining table.

At about this time he became interested in an entirely new field, the growing of rubber in the United States. "I'm just starting upon one of the greatest experiments in my life," he said. "At present we import from Africa and Asia nearly all the rubber we need for our motor cars. We'd be in an awful mess if another war broke out and our rubber supplies were cut off. We must find a way to grow our own rubber without depending upon foreign help."

Edison got his idea about growing American rubber from conversations with his cronies, Henry Ford and Harvey Firestone. These two captains of industry, the maker of automobiles and the manufacturer of tires, had impressed upon him the importance of having enough rubber at all times. They discussed this subject on one of their camping trips. For several years Edison had taken these vacation trips with Ford, Firestone and one other friend, the famous naturalist John Burroughs.

These trips were a combination of boyish pranks and serious thoughts. The four gray-haired "youngsters" spent two weeks every summer in a different part of the country. At night they slept under canvas tents. In the morning they rose at six-thirty, washed at a nearby spring or brook, ate a hearty breakfast, and went off on a "get-acquainted" tramp amidst the rocks, flowers and creatures of the woods. And on their return, they gathered around a campfire and exchanged their ideas about business, politics, life, and the great Mystery Story of the Universe.

One of Edison's chief amusements during his vacations was to experiment with all sorts of growing things in order to discover whether they contained rubber. He tried fourteen thousand different plants, from azaleas to zinnias, and found about six hundred whose juices could be manufactured into rubber. Finally he narrowed the field down to one plant, the simple goldenrod.

And thus he entered upon still another activity. He became a farmer. He began to raise goldenrod and nursed it until it grew to a height of twelve feet. He was engaged in this and in other experiments at Fort Myers, Florida, on his eighty-first birthday.

When a reporter asked him about his progress with the goldenrod, he replied: "Give me five years more, and the United States will have a rubber crop big enough to meet all our needs."

And he meant to do it! His mind still retained its old-time vigor. He tackled the problem of rubber as persistently as he had tackled all the problems of his earlier days. He regarded his gray hairs merely as a protective covering, like snow over a winter field. "It helps to keep my heart warm."

In addition to his goldenrod experiments, Edison had a bookful of notes to keep him busy, as he said, "for a hundred years." His interest in "everything" had even carried him into the field of education. He often discussed this subject with his companions during their camping trips. As a result of these discussions, he prepared the famous Edison Questionnaire.

At first this questionnaire was designed to test the knowledge of the young men who applied to him for a job. "When I call upon one of my men for a decision," he said, "I want it right away. And the promptness of his decision depends upon the ability of his memory to call upon the knowledge that is stored in his mind."

And so he prepared a number of questions, or memory and intelligence tests, for his applicants. These questions covered all sorts of subjects—geography, history, arithmetic, music, biography, art, science, commerce, and current events. And Edison insisted upon a good grade from those who wanted to work for him. He was determined to surround himself with none but the best brains.

One day, as he was discussing his questionnaire with his friends, Henry Ford suggested that it might be a good idea to offer a free college education to the student who gave the best answers. Edison adopted the idea and selected Ford as one of the judges. The other judges were Colonel Charles A. Lindbergh, George Eastman, who had helped Edison with the invention of motion-picture films, Dr. Samuel W. Stratton, president of the Massachusetts Institute of Technology, and Dr. Lewis Perry, headmaster of Phillips Exeter Academy.

The winner in the first contest was Wilbur B. Huston, a boy of sixteen who made a score of 92. Three other candidates did so well that they, too, received four-year scholarships at Edison's expense.

Another achievement by the man who was interested in "everything." A number of polls were conducted by various newspapers to determine the ten greatest living Americans. Among the men selected in most of the papers were Thomas A. Edison, Charles Evans Hughes, Herbert Hoover, Henry Ford, William Howard Taft, General John J. Pershing, Elihu Root, Booth Tarkington, John D. Rockefeller, and Charles W. Eliot.

On one of these names there was no difference of opinion. Practically all the papers picked Thomas A. Edison as the greatest American of them all.

Chapter 18

"IT IS VERY BEAUTIFUL
OVER THERE"

THE LAST YEARS of Edison's life were full of
honors. President Coolidge awarded him the Congressional Gold Medal and referred to him as "the noble,
kindly servant of the United States and benefactor of
mankind." An expedition to the South Pole set up a
beacon bearing his name on the Antarctic continent.
The Post Office Department issued a special stamp with
a picture of the first Edison electric bulb. And Henry
Ford constructed at Dearborn, Michigan, a duplicate
of Edison's original laboratory and machine shops at

Menlo Park. This new laboratory had the same equipment as the old, and even the grounds upon which it
stood were covered with several carloads of red New
Jersey clay.

When the laboratory was finished, it was dedicated
as a lasting memorial to Edison's achievements. The
dedication took place on October 21, 1929, the fiftieth
anniversary of the electric light. This occasion marked
the greatest honor that ever came to Edison. He and his
wife had been invited to Dearborn a few days before the
anniversary. He was amazed and delighted to see his
old "workshop" brought back to life. Everything in this
place was an exact replica of the original—the long
tabernacle-shaped laboratory, the shops, the red clay
that had caked his shoes so often in the past, the tables
piled with all sorts of material for experiments, the old
telegraph transmitters and crude telephones, the first
vote recorder, the little black box in which he had
generated the mysterious "etheric force," even down to
the chair and roll-top desk he had used at Menlo Park.

"Well, Tom," asked Henry Ford, "how does it strike
you?"

Edison brushed a tear from his eye, and then he said
in a voice that trembled ever so slightly: "It's ninety-
nine and nine-tenths per cent perfect!"

"What about the other one-tenth of one per cent?"

"Our floor at Menlo Park was never as clean as this!"

When they went outside, it was raining. Edison, as
usual, walked bareheaded and with his coat unbut-
toned. His wife tried to fasten his coat, but he gently

brushed her hand aside. "Don't baby me, please," he said. "I'm only eighty-two, and I feel as young as ever."

As the day of the dedication approached, Edison became somewhat restless. "I can't say that I don't enjoy all this," he said, "but I'd like to get it over and go back to my job." He was in the midst of his rubber experiments, and he begrudged any kind of interference with his work.

Yet he fell into the spirit of the occasion when the distinguished guests from all over the world began to arrive. He met President and Mrs. Hoover on the Presidential train and joined them together with the reporters and Secret Service men, as they transferred to a queer contraption of a vehicle. It was a replica of the train on which Edison had worked as a boy—two passenger cars and a baggage car drawn by a wood-burning locomotive. In the baggage car he found a basket filled with fruits and candy. Placing it over his arm, he went through the train and peddled his wares to the passengers as in the old days.

And then came the dedication and the dinner. Never in American history had so distinguished a gathering paid homage to a private citizen. The homage came not only from those present, but from many others both in America and abroad, including the Prince of Wales, President Hindenburg of Germany, Commander Richard E. Byrd, who was away on his Antarctic expedition, and Albert Einstein, who spoke his greetings from across the sea.

In the midst of the banquet there was a ceremony

that re-enacted the birth of the electric light at Menlo
Park. At a given signal the restored laboratory at Dearborn, which up to that moment had been lighted by
candles and gas lamps, burst suddenly into "electric
sunshine." And at that selfsame moment, thousands of
homes and streets and city squares throughout the nation flared into an answering salute of golden light.

When the ceremony was over, the guests paid their
separate tributes to the great inventor. President
Hoover made the principal speech. "Our scientists and
inventors," he said, "are among our most priceless national possessions . . . Mr. Edison, by his own genius and
effort, rose from a modest beginning to membership
among the leaders of men. His life gives renewed con-
fidence that our institutions hold open the door of opportunity to all those who would enter . . ."

At the end of the President's speech, Edison stood up.
He looked pale—he had just gone through one of the
most strenuous days in his life. "This experience," he
said in a voice quivering with emotion, "makes me
realize as never before that Americans are sentimental.
This crowning event of light's golden jubilee fills me
with gratitude. I thank our President and you all. As to
Henry Ford, words are inadequate to express my feel-
ings. I can only say to you that, in the fullest and richest
meaning of the term, he is my friend. Thank you, and
good night."

In the storm of applause that followed, only a few
noticed that Edison swayed as he sat down. His wife
bent over him and then turned to the man in the next

seat. "Get a doctor, quick!" she whispered. Edison was now slumped in his chair.

The President's private physician, Dr. Joel T. Boone, happened to be among the dinner guests. He ordered Edison to take a complete rest for a few days. Henry Ford offered his home for the purpose, and President Hoover insisted upon remaining in Dearborn until the danger was passed.

Edison recovered from the illness, but his sturdy frame was beginning at last to wear out. A thorough physical checkup showed that he was suffering from a complication of diseases. He was ordered to restrict himself to a milk diet.

Yet he insisted upon going on with his work. He continued his experiments on the goldenrod, and he developed a new chemical process for vulcanizing the rubber derived from this plant.

Eighty-three years old, and he was still at his laboratory. Eighty-four, and no letup in his work. "I must spend all my life in the study of the natural laws of the universe," he told his personal physician, Dr. T. A. Gresham. "I am but a humble mechanic trying to figure out the plans of the Great Engineer."

August 1, 1931. An alarming news report—the eighty-four-year-old inventor was on the point of death. He had collapsed while working at his West Orange laboratory.

But once more, to the amazement of everybody including even his physician, he rose from his bed.

This time, however, he did not return to the laboratory. For a few weeks he took daily motor trips with his wife. Then, as the summer heat took its toll of his strength, he submitted to staying indoors. He spent his time reading, making notes, and talking about the mystery of this life and the even greater mystery of the life to come.

The summer heat had given way to the chillier days of October. And the spark of Edison's vitality kept growing colder along with the weather. On the fifteenth, the doctor told Mrs. Edison that the end was near. She went to his bedside and took his hand. He smiled as his tired eyes looked into her face.

"It is very beautiful over there," he whispered.

A few minutes later he sank into a coma. The end came on October 18, 1931, just three days before the fifty-second anniversary of his invention of the electric light.